MVFOL

D1577769

WHICH HOUSE IS MINE AGAIN?

Also by Julie Wheaton

Me, Motherhood, and a Wise Woman

WHICH HOUSE IS MINE AGAIN?

80 Questions I Never Had
'til I Moved to a Subdivision

Julie Wheaton

FLAMING HOOP PRESS
san diego

Copyright © 2021 by Julie Wheaton

All rights reserved. Thank you for complying with copyright laws by obtaining written permission from the publisher before reproducing, scanning, or distributing any part of this book. Brief quotations may be used in book reviews.

The people and events appearing in this work reflect the author's experience. Some names have been changed. Neither the publisher nor the author assumes responsibility for damages of any kind resulting from the use of the information herein. Trademarks and service marks mentioned in this work are the property of their respective registered owners.

Flaming Hoop Press | San Diego, California
FlamingHoopPress@gmail.com

Cover design by Stephanie Hannus | StephanieHannus.com
Cover photo by iStock.com/Art Wager | ArtWagerPhoto.com

Library of Congress Control Number: 2021902888

PUBLISHER'S CATALOGING-IN-PUBLICATION DATA

Names: Wheaton, Julie, author.
Title: Which house is mine again? : 80 questions I never had 'til I moved
    to a subdivision / Julie Wheaton.
Description: San Diego : Flaming Hoop Press, [2021]
Identifiers: ISBN 9780984662968 (paperback) |
    ISBN 9780984662975 (ebook)
Subjects: LCSH: Wheaton, Julie--Homes and haunts. | Suburbanites--
    California, Southern--Biography. | Suburban homes--California,
    Southern--Anecdotes. | Architecture, Domestic--California,
    Southern--Anecdotes. | LCGFT: Autobiographies. | Anecdotes.
Classification: LCC HT352.U62 C36 2021 (print) | LCC HT352.U62
    (ebook) | DDC 307.74097949--dc23

With appreciation for my neighbors,
north and south,
east and west,
past and present.

CONTENTS

4. A Close-knit Community

5. Convenient Shopping

6. Youth Sports

7. AWARD-WINNING SCHOOLS

8. SOCIAL EVENTS

- INTRODUCTION -

Look-alike Houses

When I was ten years old, I didn't know why my friends' houses looked alike, but it sure was easy to find the bathroom without having to ask. If I knew where the bathroom was in Heidi's house, I knew how to find it in Sharon's house.

Heidi and Sharon lived in a subdivision of tract houses a block away from where I lived in a custom house. On a half-acre lot in San Diego, California my parents had built their dream house. Dad was a real estate developer, and Mom had studied decorative arts at UC Berkeley, which is to say that the house was beautiful. The carpet, curtains, and upholstery all coordinated. The living room had plate glass windows and an open-beam ceiling. The kitchen cabinets were painted in trendy colors like Harvest Gold, Fiesta Orange, and Avocado Green.

Surrounding the house were fruit trees, a flower garden, and a playhouse. Next door stood an acre of uncharted sagebrush where my friends and I would make forts. Squatting under a sagebrush canopy, I had my first taste of home improvement when my best friend said we could dig a hole in our fort and use spray cement to make a pool, the one amenity my house didn't have.

In my early twenties and wanting a dream house of my own, I would take myself on dream-house drives through wealthy, coastal neighborhoods north of San Diego. Wending my way through Del Mar, Solana Beach, and Rancho Santa Fe, I'd pick out palaces from the array of custom houses and snap a Kodak photo every now and then as a reminder of my hoped-for future.

Bordering these established neighborhoods was a newer area called North City West. To me, it didn't look like a city. It had a shopping center but no central business district. Even the name, *North City West*, didn't sound rooted in local history or geography. It sounded like something plucked from a city planner's map.

At each entrance to North City West stood tall, wooden totem signs that displayed the names of various subdivisions, with arrows pointing left, right, or straight ahead. I would follow colored flags, like squares on a game board, to clusters of model homes set off by coiffed landscapes, as if built by Disney.

I didn't need to snap photos because every subdivision had a glossy, four-color brochure showing floor plans and features. The brochures called North City West a "master-planned community."

When I walked through the front door of any model home, it felt like stepping into the pages of *Better Homes & Gardens* magazine. I'd flit through every floor plan and imagine how perfect life would be with a gourmet-inspired kitchen, a lavish master suite, and a pool-sized yard. Sometimes I'd loiter in a model, as if I lived there, and I'd comment to nobody in particular about the dining room's well-crafted wainscoting or the kitchen's walk-in pantry.

Even when a friend or relative did join me for a model tour, I'd ignore any negative or cautionary comments. Mom and I once toured a grand, two-story model in a subdivision called Del Mar Place, which was, notably, nowhere near the city of Del Mar. I was busy picturing where my furniture would go when Mom said, "The interior doors are missing." I glanced around and saw that she was right. "Removing the doors," she explained, "creates the illusion of space and better flow through a house." *Huh*, I thought and went back to wondering if I had enough clothes to fill the walk-in closet.

A few minutes later, Mom said, "Look at the windows. The builder used wood frames on the front of the house, where prospective buyers will see them, but cheap, aluminum frames on the sides and back."

Window, shmindow! I thought. *What I need is space and plenty of it. Someday, I'll be hauling home pallets of products from The Price Club in a shiny Suburban filled with my future twins and triplets.*

I continued my home search (alone) and one day found myself meandering along a pleasant cul-de-sac in North City West. At the top of the cul-de-sac was a grassy, pocket-sized park with a sidewalk running through it. My eye followed the sidewalk to a new elementary school. *How perfect is this? After school, my future twins and triplets can walk home, where I'll have cookies and milk on the kitchen table.*

But wait.

If all the houses look alike, how will my kids remember which house is theirs? I shuddered at the image of my brood huddled together and crying, lost on their own street. Right then, I devised a simple solution to this potential problem: I'd put a garage-door opener in each child's backpack.

I soon realized that homes in North City West were beyond my budget, so I bought a one-bedroom condo in a subdivision thirty minutes away called Avocado Village. Since then, I've lived in four more subdivisions with four meaningless names. And while I didn't have twins or triplets, I did raise three sons—Big, Middle, and Little—with my husband, Michael.

I'd lived in tract houses for ten years when I came across a phrase that worried me: Architecture influences behavior. My first concern was for my kids. *Would they turn out different somehow for being raised in a cookie-cutter house instead of a custom house?* Then I wondered, *Does a cookie-cutter house even qualify as architecture?*

Big, Middle, and Little seemed well adjusted, so I decided this maxim was probably meant for churches, stadiums, or other places where influencing behavior was important.

But I was wrong.

Subdivision living *had* affected someone's behavior: mine. For years, I'd been making up words, rationales, and workarounds, trying to tweak cookie-cutter culture to suit my sensibilities.

Tract home builders like to dream up ridiculous phrases to describe homes whose defining characteristic is sameness. They cloak basic features in fancy terms, making it hard for buyers and renters to compare apples to apples. I would deconstruct their phrases and discover that a "cultured marble Pullman top" is just a bathroom counter. A "stunning family retreat" is basically a TV room. And, "scenery reminiscent of a fabled past" is a phrase probably swiped from a romance novel and slipped into a subdivision brochure.

What I would describe as "a look-alike house on a dirt lot," a builder describes as "a coveted residence with a pool-sized yard in a close-knit community that offers convenient shopping, youth sports, award-winning schools, and social events." If that's accurate, then why don't the builders live here? My current subdivision was built by Pardee Homes, but I've never met Mr. or Mrs. Pardee or had the Pardee kids trick-or-treat at my house.

I moved to this Pardee subdivision in North City West (which had since been renamed "Carmel Valley") after Michael and I closed escrow on a twelve-year-old, Tudor-inspired home. The escrow agent handed us two keys, two garage-door openers, and a stack of documents. In the stack was a copy of the Covenants, Conditions & Restrictions for our subdivision. The CC&Rs, we were told, would answer any questions, and for more information, we could contact the Homeowners' Association.

But my questions weren't the type answered by CC&Rs or the HOA. I wanted to know why the kids' bedrooms in my coveted residence were so small. What could I do about noise coming from all those pool-sized backyards? Why were award-winning schools motivating my kids with candy? What exactly is the master plan for this master-planned community?

I began to write down my questions, my made-up words, and my odd rationales. What emerged was part memoir and part handbook, in the same way that a tract house isn't purely one style of architecture or another. It's a mix.

———

1

The Subdivision Decision

Why did the builder name it that?

I was twenty-three and driving home from work when a billboard caught my eye. It was an ad for a new subdivision of condos. On impulse, I exited the highway and followed the trail of yellow flags, like breadcrumbs, to the top of a bluff. There, on the subdivision's welcome wall* were two words I've never seen together: Avocado Village.

On my way to the sales office, I passed pristine sidewalks lined with young trees. *Those must be the avocado trees*, I thought, a you-pick perk for residents of these San Diego condos. But where was the village? I parked and walked to the center of the subdivision, expecting to see a cluster of shops, but I found only a fenced-off pool and restrooms.

I've since learned that a subdivision's name doesn't obligate a builder in the least. *Amber Bay* or *The Groves at Echo Creek* might sound like a pre-planned paradise, but either one could be located in the desert, next to a freeway, or plunked down on a backfilled pit under high-voltage power lines.

Despite what their ads say, most subdivisions aren't newly discovered natural nirvanas tended by folks with a passion for home-building. They're mass-produced tracts with spa-like names that give hope to weary, I-want-it-all house hunters.

Builders, it seems, want house hunters to fall for the image of the perfect home in the ideal neighborhood—a fall that often starts with a scenario like this one: It's Sunday morning. I sit down

---

welcome wall (*noun*): a short, horizontal masonry structure at the entrance to a subdivision, which displays the subdivision's name.

with a cup of coffee and flip through the newspaper's real estate section. I notice a lifestyle photo of a family, much like my own, taking a walk through a wooded area along a creek. The photo is part of an ad for a new subdivision of three- and four-bedroom homes.

"Honey?" I shout to Michael. "Have you seen any groves near that new mall?"

"Groves?" asks Michael. "Of what?"

"I'm not sure. This place is called The Groves at Echo Creek."

"Sounds nice," he says. "What's it like?"

I read aloud, "Welcome to exceptional living. The Groves at Echo Creek is an exclusive enclave of 243 architecturally inspired homes situated on the shores of serene Echo Creek and bordered by groves of protected trees. These new, handsomely appointed, luxurious estate-home residences boast a plethora of amenities in a country-like setting. The community's premier clubhouse is replete with a resort-style pool and a state-of-the-art fitness center. Walk to award-winning schools, and enjoy convenient shopping minutes away. Discover the life you're meant to live at The Groves at Echo Creek, where freeway-close meets country-quiet.

"Hmm," I say. "I wonder what kind of groves it has. Apples? Oranges? Peaches? I've always wanted to live in the country. Just think, we could pick fruit for breakfast and catch fish from the creek for dinner. The kids would love it! Let's take a drive, and check it out."

So we pile the kids into the squirt hauler* and take three major freeways before arriving at The Groves at Echo Creek. Here's what we find: Four homes have been built as models. The creek is a cement-lined ditch that runs past the sales office before it bee-lines to the subdivision's perimeter. Of the 243 homes, ten will have a peek of the creek. They've been christened as "creekside

---

*squirt hauler (*noun*): the family car.

homes" and priced to include a wilderness premium.* The groves are specks of non-buildable land dotted with saplings. Once the kids leave for college, the trees will be tall enough to climb.

Michael and I stare at the subdivision map like it's a geometry test. How will we determine which lot is the best lot? Unable to tap our high-school math skills, we search for a lucky-number clue.

"Maybe Lot 5 would be the best," I say. "We were married on the fifth."

"Lot 28 looks a little bigger," Michael says. "Didn't we meet at twenty-eight?"

"Oh my gosh!," I shriek. "Look at Lot 157. It's a pie-shaped lot on a double cul-de-sac.* That's it! That's the ONE!" (Finding a pie-shaped lot on a double cul-de-sac is like getting Yahtzee on the first roll.)

We quickly tell the sales agent to reserve Lot 157. She lowers her voice, as if sharing a secret, and says, "Oh, Lot 157 is *very* popular. We've had several inquiries about it, just today." This is her canned response to every buyer about every lot. She suggests we arrive a night or two before next weekend's release date, to secure a top spot on the waiting list. She's implying that we should cram the kids and the camp gear into the squirt hauler and head out for a night under the stars on the curbs of Echo Creek.

---

wilderness premium (*noun*): a surcharge on the price of a new tract home, which supposedly reflects the home's prime location as having a view of nature.

double cul-de-sac (*noun*): two adjacent dead ends, which form a street configuration resembling Mickey Mouse's ears; also, the most sought-after street configuration in a subdivision.

Subdivision Names

Builders would like me to believe that bestowing a name on a sub-division is all about the fine art of branding. Perhaps. But it's also simple enough for a seven-year-old to do.

From what I've seen, a subdivision has either a standard name (two words) or an enhanced name (three or more words). Using the table on the next page, I can create a standard name by picking a word from column 1 and a word from column 2, like this:

Dover + Heights = Dover Heights

Quail + Prairie = Quail Prairie

To craft an enhanced name, I simply join two standard names with *at*, like this:

Carriage Park at Windswept Trails

Windswept Trails at Carriage Park

Certain words in column 1 can be modified to anchor a sub-division name to ancient history. This supposed link to the past lends a pedigree, of sorts, as if prized architectural elements are being resurrected in a crop of cookie-cutter homes. To anchor a name, I add *-hurst* or *-haven* to the first word, like this:

Carriage*hurst* Park

Quail*haven* Prairie

SUBDIVISION NAMES

COLUMN 1	COLUMN 2	COLUMN 1	COLUMN 2
Alta	Acres	Pacific	Landing
Amber	Bay	Ponderosa	Lane
Arroyo	Bluff(s)	Prescott	Manor
Bayside	Bridge	Quail	Meadow(s)
Bella	Canyon	Quarry	Moor
Blossom	Common(s)	Rancho	Oaks
Bridle	Country	Scenic	Park
Brook	Cove	Shadow	Paseo
Carmel	Creek	Shimmering	Pines
Carriage	Crest	Sierra	Place
Copper	Crossing	Silhouette	Plantation
Costa	Estate(s)	Singing	Point(e)
Cottonwood	Falls	Sky	Pond
Creekside	Farm(s)	Sol	Prairie
Dover	Field(s)	Sterling	River
Eagle	Foothills	Stone(y)	Run
Echo	Forest	Sun	Square
Emerald	Garden(s)	Sundance	Terrace
Golden	Glen	Sunflower	Tides
Heritage	Green(s)	Sunset	Trail(s)
Holly	Grove(s)	Terra	Valley
Huntington	Haven	Torrey	View
Lakeshore	Heights	Trellis	Village
Mandolin	Highlands	Vista	Walk
Mill	Hill(s)	Westside	Wind(s)
Mission	Knoll(s)	Windswept	Woods

Floor-Plan Names

Creating floor-plan names is even easier than creating subdivision names. Using the table on the next page, I can create a floor-plan name by selecting a word from column 1 and a word from column 2, like this:

The + Darlington = The Darlington

I can also use a column 2 word to create an enhanced subdivision name. To do this, I accent a standard name with a column 2 word, like this:

Darlington at Windswept Trails

Windswept Trails at Darlington

Concord at Carriage Park

Carriage Park at Concord

However beautiful and timeless they seem, floor-plan names have a very short lifespan. All appear in brochures, and a lucky few are emblazoned on plaques and posted outside of model homes. But I have yet to hear homeowners refer to their floor plan by name. They usually describe it by room configuration: "My floor plan is the one with the full bathroom downstairs."

FLOOR-PLAN NAMES

COLUMN 1	COLUMN 2	COLUMN 1	COLUMN 2
The	Aberdeen	The	Grant
The	Ashley	The	Hamilton
The	Aspen	The	Hanover
The	Atrium	The	Kensington
The	Atwater	The	Kent
The	Barcelona	The	Kinsley
The	Barker	The	Langford
The	Bayberry	The	Lenox
The	Bellevue	The	Lexington
The	Bennett	The	Lincoln
The	Berkshire	The	Madison
The	Brighton	The	Mandolin
The	Buckingham	The	Mansfield
The	Burke	The	Milburn
The	Cézanne	The	Monet
The	Clement	The	New Haven
The	Concord	The	Picasso
The	Coral	The	Presidio
The	Corbin	The	Providence
The	Crawford	The	Rembrandt
The	DaVinci	The	Sapphire
The	Darlington	The	Tahoe
The	Dartmouth	The	Tapestry
The	Devon	The	Waterford
The	Eisenhower	The	Weston
The	Fillmore	The	Windsor

Who's lying when friends say they're "building a house"?

From the front yard of my Tudor-inspired tract house, I noticed a family touring the rental across the street. I recognized them from Little League games, so I went over to say hello and to ask if they were planning to move.

"Just temporarily," said the wife. "We're building a house." *Wow! That's impressive,* I thought. This well-dressed couple was in remarkable cosmetic condition, not a scratch or a splash of paint that I could see. I wondered, *How does he work construction all day and still have the hands of a software engineer? How does she hang drywall and still keep her French-manicured gel nails looking flawless?*

Other couples I knew had recently mentioned they were building a house. All were my same age and stage: married with young children. *How and when had these couples learned to build a house?* I regarded them with suspicion, the same suspicion I reserve for people in multi-level marketing. So I reviewed the facts.

First, these couples appeared to be emotionally stable. Absent was the marital strife that often accompanies homebuilding.

Second, I was familiar enough with the local area to know that the city where these couples were building homes didn't exist. In fact, it sounded remarkably like a subdivision name.

Third, I'd see these couples regularly at school fundraisers, the mall, and youth sports. From what I understand, building a home requires long days.

My findings pointed to a new possibility: Was this chic couple leveraging their obvious skill in wardrobe building to now build a house?

Wardrobe building had been drastically simplified a generation ago by Garanimals, a kids' clothing line of mix-and-match pieces. Young kids could coordinate outfits from pre-selected selections and gain self-confidence by dressing themselves. With Garanimals, stylish parents could avoid accessorizing their own highly curated look with a four-year-old wearing cowboy boots and Spiderman pajamas.

Perhaps my fashionable friends with their silky-smooth hands had been Garanimals kids. They weren't *physically* building a home, as I'd assumed. They were coordinating a home from pre-selected floor plans, features, and finishes offered by a subdivision builder.

📋 *WHAT THE AD SAYS:*

"Dual pantries"

✍ *WHAT IT REALLY MEANS:*

Each co-borrower gets a pantry.

Can I use my feet to estimate square footage?

Michael's job was once relocated from California to Washington State, and we had to move within ninety days. I browsed rental listings but had trouble visualizing square footage. Tell me a kitchen is 200 square feet, and watch me try to extrapolate using my feet.

The measurement I really needed was butts. Call it a "three-butt kitchen," and right away, I know its capacity: The kitchen can accommodate three people with one butt each *or* one person with three butts *or* a family of two one-butted adults and two kids with a half butt each. Nothing confirms room capacity faster than accidentally bumping butts with someone.

The furniture industry uses the human backside as a standard of measure, so why don't homebuilders? When I was shopping for dining chairs, I went to consignment stores and department stores. I noticed that older chairs tended to have smaller seats than those made after the popularity of high-fructose corn syrup.

Homebuilders could do me a favor by also describing foyers in terms of butts. Calling it a "generous foyer" tells me nothing. Calling it a "four-butt foyer" would let me know that my future foyer will never feel crowded if I schedule guest arrivals and departures in four-butt waves.

———

What's *not* shown a floor-plan map?

The first time I saw the terms *walk-in closet* and *walk-in pantry* on a floor-plan map, I reacted with glee. I couldn't possibly need more space than that for my food and clothing, right? On the model tour, I'd inspect a walk-in closet or a walk-in pantry by peeking in and nodding, like I was some sort of expert.

As my family, food supply, and wardrobe grew, I realized that *walk-in* is a relative term. Food for my family of five could reduce a walk-in pantry to a reach-in pantry. My wardrobe might morph a small walk-in closet into a clothing cave.*

Now, I verify all walk-in spaces by actually walking in. I enter a walk-in closet, remove my shoes, and count off how many pairs the closet can hold. I pretend to get dressed and note whether my hands hit a shelf or touch the ceiling. Inside a walk-in pantry, I squat and reach for an invisible bag of dog food, paying attention to what my rump bumps into on its way down.

If walk-in spaces are so desirable, why don't builders label *all* walk-in spaces on their floor-plan maps? The reason is that certain spaces, such as foyers and guest bathrooms, are assumed to be walk-in spaces. Unscrupulous builders use this to their advantage. I've never seen the term *walk-in foyer* on a floor-plan map, but I have been in model homes where I had to cram myself into a flea-sized foyer that could barely accommodate a toddler wearing a winter coat.

---

clothing cave (*noun*): a storage space advertised as a walk-in closet, which becomes cramped and dark after an actual wardrobe is moved in; may require minor spelunking to coordinate an outfit or find matching shoes.

I've also never seen the term *walk-in guest bath*, but I know not all guest bathrooms are walk-ins. Some are squeeze-ins. A squeeze-in guest bath has an entry door that doesn't open fully because it's blocked by the toilet, the vanity, or a low-hanging light fixture.

———

WHAT THE AD SAYS:

"Flexibly designed floor plans with flex spaces"

WHAT IT REALLY MEANS:

The floor-plan map comes with a pencil, so you can decide what to call each space.

Why is the master bedroom's closet staged with kids' clothing?

Unscrupulous builders sometimes hire unscrupulous home stagers. I was inside a model home, verifying the master bedroom's walk-in closet, when I saw a short stack of folded sweaters. I peeked at the tags. YOUTH LARGE. The closet had been staged with kids' clothing to make it feel more spacious.

Now, I pay closer attention to the size of items used in staged homes. Is the "oversized" pantry staged with Costco quantities or travel sizes? Is the "spacious" family room staged with a sofa from Pottery Barn Kids? Does the "ample" coat closet contain seventeen ski parkas or seven rain ponchos? Given the shrinking square footages of newer tract homes, I might have to downsize before I can upgrade.

———

📄 *WHAT THE AD SAYS:*

"Accommodates on-the-go families and their laid-back, flip-flops philosophy."

〰 *WHAT IT REALLY MEANS:*

The mini mudroom is too small for boots, but it has enough space for sandals.

Is a dining nook the same as a dining area?

Subdivision builders are fond of burying basic features under an avalanche of nouns and adjectives. This leaves house hunters, like me, digging through the rubble in order to compare features. Were I to show up, unannounced, at a builder's office, I'd shout like a bank robber, "Take out a sheet of paper! We're having a pop quiz." Then I'd read aloud the following statements:

1. A "convenient family-friendly dining space"…
   a) Describes a table at McDonald's.
   b) Describes a dining nook.
   c) Describes a dining area.
   d) Describes a dining room.

2. A "deluxe laundry package"…
   a) Comes with a bow.
   b) Describes a laundry center.
   c) Describes a laundry area.
   d) Describes a laundry room.

The counterforce to all of this feature creep is feature finesse, the ability to identify subtle differences between similar-sounding features. To hone my feature finesse, I outlined the nuances that differentiate nooks, areas, centers, and rooms.

The Dining Nook

The term *dining nook* is a hybrid of opposites. It combines *dining room* and *breakfast nook*. Homebuilders, landlords, and real estate agents will advertise a home with a dining nook as having an "eat-in kitchen." A dining nook is common in a condo or townhouse, known among trick-or-treaters as a bite-sized home.* The typical dining nook has just enough space for two folding chairs and a wall-mounted table from Ikea. If a dining nook is staged with a tiny freestanding table, one side of the table is usually pushed up against the wall, so the wall feels like another person at the table, to downplay the sense of dining alone.

The Dining Area

A dining area is a mid-sized space that's adjacent to a room with a non-dining function, such as a living room or a great room. With no walls to define it, a dining area is easily taken over by the dominant room and often ends up as a study space, a home office, or a hobby corner. The style of eating best suited to studying, working, or pursuing a hobby is snacking, which is why dining areas are usually found in snack-sized homes.*

The Dining Room

A dining room is the largest and most formal type of dining space in a subdivision, and it's found in full-sized homes.* A dining room has three to four walls, a chandelier, and a window. Of the dining rooms I've seen, most are used seasonally or for special occasions. In the off-season, they default to storage areas for charitable donations awaiting pickup or fundraising orders awaiting delivery, such as Girl Scout cookies, gift wrap, and popcorn.

---

bite-sized home (*noun*): a condo or townhouse; named for the candy bar size that trick-or-treaters expect.

snack-sized home (*noun*): a mid-sized, detached tract house; named for the candy bar size that trick-or-treaters expect.

full-sized home (*noun*): a large, detached tract house; named for the candy bar size that trick-or-treaters expect.

The Laundry Center

A laundry center can accommodate a stackable washer and dryer but not the twenty-pound box of soap needed for so many pint-sized loads of laundry. A bifold door in a hallway or kitchen often conceals a laundry center. Even though a laundry center looks and functions more like a laundry closet, that term was probably shot down by the builder's marketing team as being too descriptive.

The Laundry Area

A laundry area is a dedicated-but-doorless space for a side-by-side washer and dryer. A laundry area is adjacent to a room with a non-laundry function, such as a garage, a mudroom, or a kitchen. In other words, what happens in the laundry area doesn't stay in the laundry area. When piles of laundry overflow in my garage laundry area, the garage gym is closed until after laundry day.

The Laundry Room

With four walls and its own door, a laundry room is the real deal. It accommodates a full-sized washer and dryer and may also have a utility sink, a folding counter, and enough space for an ironing board. The laundry room was, for decades, the largest laundry facility available in a subdivision. Then came the laundry stadium.

The Laundry Stadium

In all my years of touring model homes, I've seen just one laundry stadium. It was in a hillside subdivision of starter castles, which most trick-or-treaters ignore because castles are too far apart for efficient candy gathering. On the model tour, I stumbled into what looked like a luxury Laundromat. I counted two commercial-grade washers and dryers, one folding counter the length of a sports bar, an under-counter refrigerator, and a wide-screen TV. The laundry stadium was located strategically next to the master bedroom's dual walk-in closets, each the size of a Rodeo Drive boutique.

———

📄 *WHAT THE AD SAYS:*

"Coffee bar, in lieu of linen closet, with under-counter refrigerator and built-in Gaggenau coffeemaker"

〰 *WHAT IT REALLY MEANS:*

You were expecting a coffee bar AND a linen closet in your million-dollar tract house? Haha! No.

How do I decide on a subdivision?

I was living in my fourth subdivision and about to move to a fifth. After I narrowed my choice to three possibilities, I drove through each neighborhood at different times of the day. Two neighborhoods felt like ghost towns. The third always had kids playing on the sidewalk and parents in beach chairs on the lawn. Each time the boys and I passed by in the squirt hauler, parents would wave. We later moved to this neighborhood of Tudor-inspired houses.

I've since learned there's a more interactive way to make the subdivision decision: Visit an all-skate happy hour. A common trait in tract houses is a garage door that's more prominent than the front door. This configuration forces the driveway to function as a front porch. On warm Friday afternoons, driveways are where residents welcome the weekend with an all-skate happy hour.

All-skate means everyone is invited: current neighbors, former neighbors, family members, friends, co-workers, out-of-town visitors, and house hunters who happen to drive by. Hosts set out ice, cups, and a few chairs. Everything else arrives on a potluck basis: appetizers, drinks, more chairs, and maybe a fire ring or a blender.

Should Michael and I want to move to another subdivision, we'll likely head out on a Friday afternoon with a casserole in the backseat. We'll cruise through our preferred neighborhoods, looking for an all-skate happy hour, where we can chat with prospective neighbors and learn the pros and cons of each floor plan.

———

Is it better to live in, or look at, an ugly house?

Older subdivisions tend to offer just one architectural style. Newer subdivisions, trying to shed this cookie-cutter image, offer a choice of styles. If I dislike Colonial style, I can select the Spanish-style house. If I dislike Colonial and Spanish, maybe there's a Craftsman option. But having options creates a new problem: my view. If I dislike a particular style, I don't want to see it across the street for the next decade.

Even if I do like all three styles, I may dislike a builder's interpretation of a style. Here in San Diego, many tract home builders use brownish-orange, terra-cotta roof tiles. This Spanish-style roof looks great on a stucco house with wrought iron detailing. But a terra-cotta roof on a house with white vinyl windows? That's like bean dip with whipped cream. They're both good but not together.

So I have a choice to make: Do I live in, or look at, an ugly house? Maybe I don't have to love my home's exterior because I rarely see it. In fact, I can curate my view by living in, rather than looking at, an ugly house. If the picture window in my hideous Colonial faces a handsome Craftsman, I can create a consistently Craftsman experience by furnishing my house with Craftsman pieces to match the view.

———

2

A Coveted Residence

Where's everything I paid for?

On my first visit to Avocado Village, the sales agent handed me a brochure and pointed the way to the model tour. An outdoor staircase led to the first model, where a patio entrance lush with plants embraced me like a favorite aunt. Bushy ferns and flower blooms cascaded from colorful pots. A small ficus tree strung with tiny white lights beckoned me to the front door.

Inside the one-bedroom condo, thick carpet covered the living room. Mirrored closet doors made the bedroom feel twice as large. And the ultimate upgrade? Wallpaper in the bathroom.

In the galley kitchen, sunlight streamed through a garden window filled with knickknacks. In the kitchen's cul-de-sac, I opened a bifold door and gasped: a stackable washer and dryer. *Oh my gosh, that's sooo European!* (I've never been to Europe.)

I walked upstairs to the loft, which overlooked the living room under a sharply slanted ceiling. *This would be the perfect place for my desk.* I had found my first home.

While my real condo was under construction, I took weekly walk-throughs* of my model condo, not only to immerse myself in my dream home but also to take measurements, steal decorating ideas, and inhale that new-home smell (which I now realize was probably flame retardants and formaldehyde).

On move-in day, I dashed up the outdoor staircase, ready for a welcome-home hug from my patio entrance. What had evoked a

---

weekly walk-through (*noun*): a recurring visit to the same model home for the purposes of taking measurements, stealing decorating ideas, and locating defects; *conjugations:* bi-*weekly walk-through*, tri-*weekly walk-through*.

favorite aunt now resembled a naked uncle. Lifeless stucco walls reached to the sky. The patio floor was covered in a faux-pebble coating the color of Nacho Cheese Doritos. I opened the front door and stood there, horrified. *Where's everything I paid for?*

The condo was empty and stark. It had an echo I hadn't noticed in the model. There was no wallpaper and no knickknacks, just Rental Beige paint from top to bottom.

Over the next few months, my weekly walk-throughs jumped to bi-weekly, then tri-weekly, as I tried to ferret out why the model condo look like a page from *San Diego Home/Garden* magazine, but my real condo looked like a stick drawing on an Etch-a-Sketch.

Each time I passed through the sales office, on the way to my model,* I braced for the word I didn't want to hear: sold. Unless I befriended the buyer of my model, I'd never see the inside of it again. Secretly, I wished the builder had filmed a deckumentary* of each floor plan and given it as a housewarming gift.

––––––

 *WHAT THE AD SAYS:*

"A generous array of standard features"

WHAT IT REALLY MEANS:

Prepare to be bowled over by mediocrity.

––––––––––––

my model (*noun*): a reference made by the buyer of a new tract home to the model home with the same floor plan.

deckumentary (*noun*): a short film that documents the professional decorating process used to deck out model homes.

Was it like this in the model?

On move-in day at Avocado Village I made three post-purchase discoveries.* First, the cupboard under the kitchen sink was too small for my average-sized trash can. Since I had two dogs, the trash can would have to sit in the kitchen's cul-de-sac during the day and on the counter at night.

In the cul-de-sac, I made another post-purchase discovery: The laundry center's bifold door faced the pantry door, but the bifold door wouldn't open fully if the pantry door was also open. Because the laundry center couldn't accommodate my bulk-sized box of laundry soap, I stored the box in the pantry. Adding soap to the washing machine now required a series of carefully executed 180-degree turns, opening and closing doors.

My third post-purchase discovery? No water spigot on my upstairs patio. The model's patio jungle, I learned, was maintained by a professional plant-care service. To water my plants, I made trips to and from the kitchen sink, toting a watering can of turquoise blue Miracle Grow that splashed over the edge and onto my dove gray, economy-grade carpet.

In hindsight, I should've conducted a pre-purchase vetting by inviting family members and friends to my model condo for an informal vet-together. I could've ordered pizza for delivery and handed out Sherlock Homes hats as party favors before sending guests on a scavenger hunt to inspect my model's design elements, systems, and features. Such a fact-finding fiesta would've revealed the floor plan's quirks and eliminated post-purchase discoveries.

---

post-purchase discovery (noun): any aggravating design flaw that a buyer overlooked on the model tour and must now live with.

In *hound*sight,* I should have included my dogs in the vetting process. Weeks after moving in, I awoke one night to warm dog breath on my face. I sat up and squinted at a large, dark spot on the wall about twelve inches above the floor. I reached through the darkness to touch the spot, and my hand landed on a wall stud.

Had I taken my dogs on a weekly walk-through, I might have seen them licking the walls. I wasn't sure which pup had enjoyed a midnight snack of gypsum, until our morning walk when one dog pooped in Rental Beige.

📋 *WHAT THE AD SAYS:*

"Luxurious tile"

👓 *WHAT IT REALLY MEANS:*

All the luxury of something cold, hard, and flat.

---

houndsight (*noun*): a revised perception of the nature of a dog; usually marked by the discovery of an annoying habit.

Why do neighbors ask what I paid for my home?

As a new resident at Avocado Village, I would meet the other residents whenever our paths crossed at the mailbox, setting out trash cans, or walking dogs. Most people would introduce themselves, welcome me to the neighborhood, and then continue on their way. But certain people, particularly senior citizens, would linger. They would make small talk, and then, too soon in our conversation, they would ask what I'd paid for my condo.

I chalked up their question to rudeness until I figured out that subdivision homes are priced like airline tickets. The longer you wait to buy, the higher the price. Established residents, who can find out how much a new buyer paid, can calculate their own early-phase equity.* I was disappointed to learn how much more I'd paid for the same floor plan, until I realized I'd be in the same position after the next phase of condos was complete. What neighbors hadn't divulged was that early-phase equity isn't given. It's earned.

The garden window of my upstairs condo once overlooked a vacant lot across the street. Within months, the lot disappeared into a dust storm of home construction. Crews rolled in at dawn, power tools fired all day long, and strange vehicles blocked my garage door. I had frequent flat tires from driving over debris, and when the wind blew just right, it carried the wretched stench of Porta Potties into my home.

---

early-phase equity (*noun*): the value of ownership in a new tract home that can be attributed to price increases in subsequent phases of the subdivision.

A crust of dirt and stucco splatter encased my garden window, making it seem like nighttime all the time in my kitchen. I filled my watering can, carried it up to the loft, and stuck the nozzle through the loft's porthole. I aimed the trickle at the garden window but only made more mud.

The stress of living across the street from a construction site had me considering all kinds of coping mechanisms, such as travel, shopping, counseling, and wine. Fortunately, I was so broke from buying a home that I couldn't afford to escape. Had these coping costs hit my balance sheet, they would have quickly eroded any early-phase equity.

———

 *WHAT THE AD SAYS:*

"A rural feel"

WHAT IT REALLY MEANS:

The subdivision sits next to an area designated as Open Space on the map in the sales office. A week after you move in, the designation will change to Released for Development.

That's a vaulted ceiling?

Like my second-story condo, my Tudor-inspired, two-story house also has a sharply slanted ceiling. To builders and real estate agents, this is a vaulted ceiling. *Like a bank vault?* It didn't make sense, so I went to Dictionary.com and learned that *vault* also describes "an arched structure, usually made of stones, concrete, or bricks, forming a ceiling or roof over a hall, room, or sewer."

A vaulted ceiling supposedly adds an architectural wow factor by lending expansiveness and light to a room. Vaulted ceilings, in tract homes, seem to be reserved for foyers, living rooms, dining rooms, and master bedrooms. Bathroom ceilings are never vaulted. *But sewer ceilings are?*

When I see a phrase like "voluminous, double-height ceilings," I know it refers to a mostly one-story home offered at a two-story price. Every homeowner I've met, who has a vaulted ceiling, has considered building out the vaulted area to add square footage, without the hassle of obtaining HOA approval.

In my living room, there's nothing arched about the vaulted ceiling. Its asymmetrical design more resembles a lean-to. There's no trace of stone, concrete, or brick, just orange-peel texture.

But I've discovered a hidden feature in my vaulted ceiling: good acoustics. The ceiling's highest and best use is as a rudimentary concert shell that projects voices, music, and TV blare from the first floor into upstairs bedrooms. In the evenings, I can stand under my vaulted ceiling and calmly say, "Dinner," with no need to shout. Good acoustics would also amplify calls for help, which may explain why sewer ceilings are vaulted.

———

Why are the kids' bedrooms so small?

The kids' bedrooms in our tract house measure ninety square feet, most of it occupied by a twin bed, a desk, and a dresser. There's almost no space for Big, Middle, or Little to hang out with friends or have a sleepover.

To boost bedroom sizes, two neighbors who have my floor plan expanded their second story. That seemed like a good option, so I met with an architect. The ground floor, I learned, would have to be jackhammered and reinforced to support the extra weight. Given that Michael and I barely had an emergency fund and were way behind on saving for college, remodeling was out of reach.

When Big left for college, he settled into a dorm room that had a twin bed, a desk, and a dresser. Not once did he whine about his dime-sized accommodations.

Aha! The small-bedroom strategy was coming into focus now. The architects who designed my 1986 tract house had the foresight to understand that most middle-class parents want their kids to attend college. A college degree can confer the earning power kids will need to someday purchase their own tract house.

To prepare sprawl-town teens for dorm living, these architects designed a secret feature: the college-prep bedroom. Of course, there's no space to hang out with friends or have sleepovers because such distractions can lower a student's grade point average.

When Big boomeranged home, college degree in hand, I wondered how long he'd tolerate living in his old bedroom. Much to my surprise, the college-prep bedroom comes with an expiration date. If a college-prep bedroom is occupied by a college grad, it morphs into another secret feature: the big-city bedroom. Eventually, Big moved to a dinky, downtown apartment, again with no complaints.

Once frustrated by my home's small bedrooms, I now realize how fortunate I am to have three college-prep bedrooms that shift to big-city bedrooms, as needed.

———

 *WHAT THE AD SAYS:*

"High bedroom count"

WHAT IT REALLY MEANS:

Enough bedrooms for your high kid count.

House-training isn't just for dogs, is it?

I was walking across my driveway when I saw a man and a woman in their early thirties loitering on the driveway next door. They looked lost, so I asked, "Are you the new renters?"

"Yes," said the woman. "We're supposed to meet the property manager to get the keys. We signed our lease a month ago, but we haven't been here since. We're not sure which house is ours."

It made sense. Renters don't normally carry around a copy of their lease, but maybe they should if they've rented a look-alike house. Depending on lease terms, renters might have just six short months to become house-trained.* Homeowners generally have more time, especially if the home they buy is their funeral home.*

Michael, it turns out, takes a long time to house-train. Fortunately, the established residents on our street are happy to help. They do so by flagging down any car that whizzes past the house where it's normally parked.

———

house-trained (*adjective*): the ability to identify one's look-alike home without the aid of an electronic device, a photo, or a document.

funeral home (*noun*): the residence that one expects to live in until death.

Why would one house need two sets of driving directions?

The simple answer is that visitors from outside my master-planned community need more details than insiders do. Outsiders tend to forget that using navigation software to find a subdivision is risky at best.

For example, if I live in a subdivision called Santa Barbara, my driving directions for outsiders must clearly state that I don't live in the city of Santa Barbara, California. My subdivision is merely Santa Barbara-like, meaning it reflects an aspect of the real Santa Barbara (probably the home prices).

On the other hand, my directions for insiders must clearly state, "I live in Santa Barbara." Most insiders are familiar with the welcome walls in our community, so I need only to direct a visitor from my welcome wall to my house.

To help insiders and outsiders identify which house is mine, I'll mention a distinctive curbside feature, such as a basketball hoop or a red front door. Telling visitors to look for a white squirt hauler parked in the driveway isn't helpful since a few residents on my street also drive look-alike cars.

———

How do I let a houseguest know it's time to leave?

During a party at Melissa's tract house, I was in the guest bathroom when I noticed a cat litter box in the shower stall. Melissa lives down the street from me in a Plan 4 house, where the guest bathroom also serves the only bedroom on the ground floor. The main cluster of bedrooms is upstairs.

A ground-floor guest room with its own full bath is irresistible to out-of-town visitors, especially in-laws. Melissa's in-laws visited so often that I recognized their car. By placing a litter box in the shower stall, I surmised that Melissa had casually converted her guest suite into a guessed suite.*

Were I to do this, I'd first have to adopt a cat. Then again, cats rarely show up when they're called to meet guests, so why bother proving I have a cat?

Back at the party, I was perusing the dessert table when I saw another cat litter box *on the table*! I held my breath and went in for a closer look. The litter turned out to be crushed graham crackers. The cat poops were chocolate Tootsie Rolls. *Ha!* I wouldn't need a cat after all. With a shallow tray and two pantry items, I could whip up a maintenance-free houseguest manager in minutes.

––––––

guessed suite (*noun*): a guest bedroom and bathroom where a host has eliminated all guesswork as to how long a guest is welcome, usually by placing an obstacle to the guest's comfort, such as a cat litter box in the bathroom or too many mothballs in the closet.

Do I have to park in my garage?

A garage used only for cars is, in my experience, an under-utilized garage. We park in the driveway, so we can enjoy a modern, car-less garage.

A car-less garage is a flexible space that can fulfill the missing feature in a home's floor plan. For example, a tract home built in the 1970s wouldn't have a great room, so this home's garage might be set up as a place to relax and watch TV. A 1980s tract home wouldn't have a home office, so its car-less garage might be set up as a workspace. Over the years, our garage has been a game room, a gym, and a warehouse for several home-based businesses.

Some homeowners build a wall in the garage to create a hobby space, hair salon, music studio, boutique, or repair shop. Finding the right mix of activities is a process of trial and error. Here are combos I would avoid:

- Wine bar | Drum studio
- Sauna | Apocalypse food storage
- Hair salon | Cigar lounge
- Auto repair shop | Daycare center
- Painter's studio | Clothing boutique

Where's the best place for my home office?

In tract home architecture, the home office made a quiet debut as an invented amenity. I remember the first time I noticed it on a floor-plan map: Bedroom #3/Optional Home Office. Touring the model, I found Bedroom #3 in the kids' wing of the house. It was staged with a desk, a chair, and a cardboard computer. Bedroom #2, which should have been staged with a twin bed, a nightstand, and a dresser, had two toddler beds and a small dresser in between them that doubled as a nightstand. Bedroom #2 also shared a Jack-and-Jill bathroom with the home office. How much would I accomplish in an office next door to Middle and Little's shared bedroom?

Years later, and forgetting what I'd seen in that model home, I set up my office in a bedroom next door to Middle and Little's shared bedroom. I quickly learned that the kids' wing is the worst location for a home office. As a writer and a mom, what I needed was an office space outside my home but not too far from home. That's when I hit upon the perfect solution: locating my home office in someone else's home.

Distractions kill productivity. Having my home office in my own home means the distractions are mine, too: my dirty dishes to wash, my kids bickering, my front door to answer. If my office is in a neighbor's home, am I gonna wash their dishes? Nope. Do I care what their kids are arguing about? Not really. What are the chances that I'll answer my neighbor's front door? Zero.

When a neighbor of mine, Hal, was laid off, he set up a home office in his spare bedroom and began job hunting. Without prior telecommuting experience, Hal was unaware of the hazards lurking in his home office. Midway through a phone interview, Hal's kitten crept in and jumped onto his lap, causing Hal to leap up in surprise, which scared the kitten.

Without a tree to climb, the kitten climbed Hal. In a flash, she clawed her way up his chest and across his face. Hal continued his phone call, bleeding and balancing a kitten. How did the interview end? With a request for a face-to-face interview. Had Hal's office been in a neighbor's home, he might have avoided walking into a job interview with kitten scratches on his face.

———

📋 *WHAT THE AD SAYS:*

"CAT5 wiring system for your future communication needs"

〰 *WHAT IT REALLY MEANS:*

Wiring that is obsolete but still juts through a cable TV outlet as a wall-mounted chew toy for the cat.

How can I generate income at home after a job layoff?

Michael and I once did a cash-out refinance to remodel two bathrooms, re-face the kitchen cabinets, and replace the carpet in our living room. We signed contractor agreements, and the next day, Michael was abruptly downsized out of his job as a sales rep. I wondered how we might generate income from a home with updated bathrooms, refaced cabinets, and new carpet, without having to move.

Since we both work from home, I imagined us offering a one-day workshop to on-site employees who want to learn the basics of telecommuting. And where better to try telecommuting than in a suburban tract house with a family of five?

As a place of business, our house would need a proper name, so I crafted a subdivision name and tacked on the words *conference center*. The result, Pacific Pines Conference Center, conveyed just the right mix of business complexity and golf course serenity. I then wrote copy for an imaginary brochure (mostly as a creative outlet to relieve the stress of job hunting, home remodeling, and having three kids at home for the summer).

❖ Pacific Pines Conference Center ❖

Want to reduce your overhead by having certain employees telecommute? Identify your most promising prospects with our Try Telecommuting seminar, a one-day, total-immersion event held at a fully functioning suburban home complete with a family of five.

Your team will start the day with telecommuting basics like how to select a waist-up wardrobe for video meetings, how to camouflage barking and screaming, and how to prioritize when the doorbell, the landline, and a cell phone ring at the same time. Select our Signature Premier Add-on Package, and we'll share life-tested tips on how to deal with door-to-door solicitors and what to do when a neighbor shows up holding four foster puppies.

At midday, your team will head to our gourmet galley kitchen, where they will find last night's take-out food and just enough cheese to make a low-calorie quesadilla. They can enjoy lunch in our formal dining room, on the patio, or in the breakfast nook. When that two o'clock slump hits, team members can claim one of four couches for a quick siesta or brew a Nespresso before facing advanced telecommuting challenges, like these:

• Mastering no-fail mute button strategies

• Staying on task while chainsaws roar in a neighbor's yard

• Cleaning up fast after pet accidents in a home office

• Working around feng shui cures placed by a thoughtful spouse

By day's end, you'll know which employees can telecommute full time, part time, or not at all.

Call today for a tour, and we'll send you a garage-door opener, so you'll know which ~~house~~ conference center is ours.

How do I make my look-alike house stand out?

Home décor magazines and TV shows offer plenty of advice on how to make my cookie-cutter house stand out from surrounding houses. Paint is the number one suggestion. A unique color, they say, will make my house "pop."

Years ago, our owners* had painted the body of the house in butter yellow and the trim in Kelly green. The colors popped, but it wasn't a pretty pop, especially on a Tudor-inspired exterior. Both colors were, by now, badly faded, so I had two options for creating a standout house: I could repaint or flee paint.

Were I to repaint in a snazzy color scheme, the house would stand out but only until neighbors copied the scheme. Were I to flee paint, the house's deferred-maintenance patina would gain complexity, making it a standout that no one could copy. Strict enforcement of CC&Rs makes deferred maintenance a rare victory in a subdivision.

A professional painter was working across the street one day, so I asked for his opinion: Did my house need repainting? "No," he said. "It just needs pressure-washing."

On a Saturday, Michael and I rented a pressure washer and watched as our home revealed its palette from the past: a brighter butter yellow, a deeper Kelly green, and suddenly, a bonus color—gray polka dots where the high-powered water had ripped off patches of stucco.

---

our owners (*plural noun*): a reference made by the present owners of a tract home to the home's previous owners.

Ugly, yes. But also eye-catching and unique. No other house in the subdivision had gray polka dots. The next day, record-setting wildfires charred a region of San Diego and smothered our house in ash, making it look like all the others again.

———

 WHAT THE AD SAYS:

"Built-in fireplace with wine grotto"

WHAT IT REALLY MEANS:

For those who like a good char on their chardonnay.

Is my house eligible for a TV makeover show?

On a street of look-alike houses, even a minor makeover can help residents remember which house is theirs. Were my house to be picked for a show like HGTV's *Curb Appeal*, I can only imagine the exciting changes the designers would make. New landscaping? Stylish house numbers? An inviting walkway? I explored the prospect of submitting my house for consideration, and what I learned can be summed up in a simple equation where,

$$1 \text{ HOA} + 1{,}000 \text{ CC\&Rs} = 0 \text{ appearances on HGTV}$$

That is, homes governed by an HOA and subject to CC&Rs are usually ineligible for TV makeover shows because changes to a home's exterior must be pre-approved by the HOA's Architectural Improvement Committee. This handful of homeowners appears to have a sworn duty to protect neighborhood neutrality.* From what I've read, the approval process is so slow and cumbersome that HGTV rarely considers cookie-cutter houses for makeover shows.

————

————

neighborhood neutrality (*noun*): the bland color palette of a typical subdivision, emanated by earth-toned houses, brown roofs, and beige walls.

3

A Pool-sized Yard

How large is a pool-sized yard?

"HUGE VIEW LOT!" the ad read, so I went to the Open House. I walked in the front door, headed to the backyard, and discovered this wasn't a huge view lot. It was a huge-view lot. A huge view lot (no hyphen) is a big lot with a view. A huge-view lot is a small lot with a view that belies its small size. This particular huge-view lot overlooked a four-lane highway, wetlands, an eight-lane freeway, more wetlands, and the county fairgrounds. That *is* a huge view.

In my master-planned community, very few lots strike me as huge. The lot beneath my detached, single-family home is 4,900 square feet, but builders and real estate agents have no qualms about advertising lots of this size as having a pool-sized yard, an estate-sized yard, or a family-sized yard. To decode these nebulous terms, I rely on my feature finesse.

A Pool-sized Yard

When I first saw the term *pool-sized yard*, I pictured a backyard with plenty of space for an Olympic-sized, resort-style pool, a hot tub, and a cabana. Then I toured a few pool-sized yards and realized that *pool-sized* refers to another kind of resort-style pool: the kiddie pool.

Once a pool-sized yard has fulfilled its potential, the yard is then advertised as having a "backyard pool," where *yard* is the adjective, and *pool* is the noun. That is, all pool and no yard.

An Estate-sized Yard

The term *estate-sized yard* seemed to swoop in and replace *pool-sized yard* during the Great Recession, when any reference to water—

particularly being underwater on a mortgage—became politically incorrect. The estate-sized yards I've seen are under-landscaped or unmaintained backyards used by the residents to store items that won't fit inside the ~~house~~ estate.

The ad for an estate-sized yard will often say, "Plenty of space for all your toys!" This is correct. With no flower beds to trample or trees to dodge, this dirt lot provides direct access to trailers, boxes, bins, and bags.

A Family-sized Yard

A family-sized yard is similar to an estate-sized yard, but it also has a flat, bare spot suitable for an accessory dwelling unit to house a grandparent, a returning college grad, or a high-maintenance teen.

———

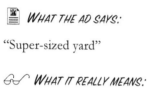 *WHAT THE AD SAYS:*

"Super-sized yard"

WHAT IT REALLY MEANS:

The yard is too small to grow your own food, but you can enjoy fast food *alfresco*.

What's a privacy barrier?

In my subdivision of single-family detached homes, five-foot-tall wood fences divide backyards and grant visual privacy to anything under sixty inches. Doghouses, barbecues, and patio storage boxes are private. Patio covers, second-story windows, and mature trees are not. Some items and activities have privacy settings that toggle:

- Sitting in the backyard is private. Standing is not.
- A pool is private. A pool slide is not.
- A playhouse is private. A tree house is not.
- A trampoline is private, but jumping on it is not.

To increase privacy, Michael and I, along with our neighbors, added a one-foot-tall privacy barrier atop our fence. The term *privacy barrier* is HOA-speak for a panel of lattice or angled wood slats, amounting to a see-through fence at eye level. Wisteria and ivy on our privacy barrier have increased opacity to 95% in some spots. As the vines have grown upward, we've gained six inches of privacy in the same way that frizzy hair makes a person appear taller.

If we ever move to a brand new subdivision with no landscaping, we'll probably do the same thing: add a privacy barrier atop the fence and then grow a privacy barrier for our privacy barrier, by starting a hedge fund.*

---

hedge fund (*noun*): money earmarked for the purchase of fencing and/or plants, usually with the intent of increasing privacy.

How far does sound travel in a subdivision?

Even a five-foot-tall fence with an ivy-filled privacy barrier is no match for intimate, late-night conversation coming from a neighbor's pool or hot tub. Sound travels so efficiently over water that I wonder why these neighbors haven't posted a shortened version of the Miranda Warning:

1. You have the right to remain silent.
2. Anything you say can be used against you.

At-risk remarks include gossip, slander, usernames, passwords, bad stock tips, romantic murmurings, offensive jokes, and political comments.

Pool or no pool, whenever I find myself in the backyard of a detached, single-family tract home, I assume a three-home radius for eavesdropping purposes. If I'm on the patio or balcony of an attached home, I assume that anything I say can be heard within a six-home radius.

———

📄 *WHAT THE AD SAYS:*

"Concrete block side yard return wall with vinyl side and rear yard fencing"

↪ *WHAT IT REALLY MEANS:*

The yard is fenced.

What's the highest and best use of my side yard?

A side yard is that strip of dirt in between tract houses, where the scaffolding once stood. My house faces east, so I have a north side yard and a south side yard. Both are five feet wide, except at the chimney bumpout, where it narrows to thirty-one inches.

In my south side yard, I hung a clothesline to conserve energy and save the planet. Over the fence, a neighbor once used her north side yard to honor nature in a different way: letting her two dogs answer the call of nature. Inches away from my clean laundry was a dog toilet.

When incompatible uses, like these, exist in neighboring side yards, the more offensive use typically prevails. In this case, the dog toilet won, and I lived with compromised use of my south side yard until that neighbor moved. Here are other incompatible uses:

- Pool heater | Meditation garden
- Pesticide storage | Playhouse
- Beehive | Tanning area
- Barbecue | Flower bed

The Dog Toilet Years were made worse by the dogs' barking in the side yard, usually during Little's nap. When I mentioned the situation to another neighbor, he offered me his ultrasonic barking deterrent. I set the small wood box atop the privacy barrier and camouflaged it with ivy.

The deterrent drove the dogs to bark on the other side of their yard, but it had zero effect on the dog toilet. At that point, I had two options for reclaiming full use of my side yard: aim higher on the list of offensive uses or switch to a more compatible use by, say, storing my trash cans in that side yard. Here are examples of other compatible uses:

- Compost heap | Vegetable garden
- Chicken coop | Fruit trees
- Barbecue | Smoker

 *WHAT THE AD SAYS:*

"Proper hose bibs"

WHAT IT REALLY MEANS:

The builder's plumber also wrote the ad copy.

Do I have to join the HOA?

At the close of escrow on our Tudor-inspired tract house, I asked the escrow agent, "Do I have to join the HOA?" The agent said I wouldn't be able to buy the house unless I joined the HOA and agreed to the subdivision's Covenants, Conditions & Restrictions (CC&Rs). I had no idea what *covenant* meant, so I opened a dictionary and found it right after *coven* (a gathering of witches).

Using monthly dues paid by homeowners, the HOA hires a property management company to administer the CC&Rs. One of the responsibilities is to maintain the subdivision's Common Area, which includes fences, landscaping, and welcome walls. The fence that runs across my backyard appeared to be a Common Area fence, so I assumed the property management company would replace one termite-eaten fence post. Here's the conversation I had when I called the HOA's management company:

RECEPTIONIST
(perky)
Hello and thank you for calling. How may I provide you with excellent service today?

ME
(also perky)
Hi, I'm a homeowner at Amber Bay, and I have a fence post that needs to be replaced due to termite damage.

RECEPTIONIST
I'll connect you with your coordinator. Please hold.

                    COORDINATOR
                    (monotone)
This is the coordinator.

                        ME
Hi, I'm a homeowner at Amber Bay, and I have
a fence post that needs to be replaced due to
termite damage.

                    COORDINATOR
That's the responsibility of the homeowner.

                        ME
                    (confused)
But what about the monthly dues I've been
paying for eight years? Don't they cover
repairs to the Common Area fence?

                    COORDINATOR
No. That's the responsibility of the
homeowner.

                        ME
            (disappointed, then curious)
Huh. Okay. Can I put in a different fence?

                    COORDINATOR
No. You have to replace exactly what's there.

                        ME
                    (defeated)
Yeah, I suppose so. Okay, give me the phone
number of the company that handles these
repairs, and I'll take care of it.

                    COORDINATOR
That's the responsibility of the homeowner.

                    ME
                (explosive)
What?!

                    COORDINATOR
That's the responsibility of the homeowner.

                    ME
                (feigning calm)
You're kidding, right?

                    COORDINATOR
No. That's the responsibility of the
homeowner.

                    ME
                (angry)
Let me make sure I understand this. You won't
replace the fence post, but I'm required to.
You won't tell me where to buy a replacement
post, but I'm legally bound to repair the
post according to your standards. Not only
will you *not* help me do this correctly but if
I do it incorrectly, you can and will put a
lien on my property.

                    COORDINATOR
That's correct.

                            ———

📄 *WHAT THE AD SAYS:*

"Interior lot"

✍ *WHAT IT REALLY MEANS:*

A viewless homesite in the middle of a subdivision

The HOA says I'm in non-compliance. Is that good or bad?

As a first-time buyer at Avocado Village, I couldn't afford window coverings for my new condo, so I hung sheets and towels. Weeks later, the HOA sent a Notice of Non-compliance to inform me that, "Towels, sheets, and painter's plastic are not approved window coverings."

I pulled out my well-worn credit card and ordered aluminum mini blinds. It took two weeks for the blinds to arrive, two days to install them, and a few hours for my two dogs to chew them up while I was at work one day. The blinds still functioned, so I remained not in non-compliance.

To the HOA, a resident is either "in non-compliance" (wrong) or "not in non-compliance" (not wrong). Said another way, the highest level of compliancy is to be not wrong.

Remaining not wrong means not breaking the rules but not following them, either. A teenager in my current master-planned community was nearly cited by the city for hanging a tire swing from a tree in a public park near his house. The swing supposedly blocked the public right-of-way.

Because the neighborhood kids enjoyed the swing, this enterprising teen made sure the swing was never in place long enough to generate a citation. He'd climb the tree twice a day—once, to hang the swing, and again, to take it down.

After the HOA sent us a Notice of Non-compliance, for our freestanding basketball hoop in the street, we borrowed a page from the teenager's playbook. Michael and the boys dragged the hoop to our driveway. I signed the Response to Inspection Letter, confirming the hoop was no longer in the street. A few days later, we moved the hoop back to the street, committing a fresh, new violation.

📄 *WHAT THE AD SAYS:*

"Experience a dynamic lifestyle close to neighborhood parks, a solar-heated swimming pool, and a community fitness center."

☞ *WHAT IT REALLY MEANS:*

These amenities aren't in the subdivision. They're close to it.

How do I buy time to correct a violation?

The HOA once sent us a Notice of Non-compliance for having a dirt patch in our front yard. Michael had prepared the soil for two fruit trees and would be buying the trees that next weekend. The patch had been there only a few days when, apparently, the HOA board members conducted an impromptu inspection and cited us.

Michael covered the patch in bark chips, and I signed the Response to Inspection Letter, restoring our status to not in non-compliance. It was an easy fix, but what if future violations are beyond the scope of bark chips as a remedy? How do we appease the HOA and buy time? We do it the HOA way: We post a sign.

To announce its upcoming meeting, the HOA posts a sign. To remind residents to park in their driveway on street-cleaning day, the HOA posts a sign. To keep people and dogs off the grass in a pocket park, the HOA posts a lawn sign like this one: "Pardon the inconvenience. Landscape renovation in progress." Had the HOA board members seen a contractor's lawn sign in our dirt patch, they might have nodded and moved on, reassured that trained professionals would be handling the forthcoming improvements.

I wonder if we can ward off future citations by permanently posting a contractor's lawn sign. On second thought, why clutter our yard when I can just snap a photo of a contractor's sign in a neighbor's yard? If the HOA sends a Notice of Non-compliance, I can submit the photo as a way of saying, "We're working on it." One advantage of look-alike houses is that the HOA probably can't remember which house is mine, either.

———

Can I negotiate with the HOA?

In my subdivision of single-family houses, adding a non-approved sunroom is a major violation of the CC&Rs. A minor violation might be painting a home's exterior trim in teal. One homeowner committed both of these violations, and predictably, he received a Notice of Non-compliance.

But wait.

Isn't the homeowner *also* a member of the group that sent the notice? Bingo! Every homeowner in the subdivision is a member of the group that sent the notice. Having an HOA is like paying someone to protect me from myself. If I don't do what I agreed to do, then the HOA has my permission to take away my stuff.

Savvy residents use this double-agent status as leverage. The homeowner with the teal trim argued that, since his sunroom wasn't visible from the street, it posed no disruption to neighborhood neutrality. The teal trim, being clearly visible, was disruptive to the earth-toned palette of surrounding houses. So the homeowner struck a deal with the HOA. In exchange for retroactive approval of his sunroom, he painted his trim in a neutral color.

———

Where should I hide my spare house key?

Because cookie-cutter homes are identical, first-time buyers might assume there's a master key. If these newcomers lock themselves out, they might call the neighborhood security guard when they should be calling a locksmith.

A cheaper backup plan is to trade keys with a trusted neighbor, but I've seen this unfold in unexpected ways. When a teenager on my street was locked out, he walked to his friend's house to ask for the spare key. That's when he realized his friend's family had just left for a two-week vacation. The teen didn't know how to break into his own house, but he did know how to break into his friend's house and where the spare key was kept.

This left me wondering about the best spot to hide a spare key. Hiding it in my own yard is too obvious, but hiding it inside a neighbor's house carries certain risks. What if I combined these strategies and hid my key in a neighbor's yard? Thieves want quick access and convenience. Hiding my key six houses away is a huge hassle for the average thief. But what if my six-houses-away neighbor discovers my key while doing yard work? He'll probably think it's a key *he* hid long ago, and he'll re-hide it in the same place.

I'm not keen on trespassing, so a better option might be a magnetic, hide-a-key holder that I smack to the underside of a mailbox down the street. To avoid any trouble with the Postal Service, I'd add a stamp. Then, if a family member gets locked out, I can text him a house number rather than a long description involving a rock or a flowerpot in a neighbor's yard. This plan also lets me verify my key's presence periodically with a quick sweep of the hand during an evening walk.

I like this idea even more than a keyless strategy I once used: leaving my front door wide open for hours in broad daylight. (I exited my house through the garage and forgot to close the front door.) To a thief, this must mean that someone is home and forgot to close the door or that the home has been burglarized and the good stuff is already gone.

———

 *WHAT THE AD SAYS:*

"A sister community"

WHAT IT REALLY MEANS:

The key to the subdivision's residents-only pool and clubhouse was given to 386 other households in the neighboring, or sister, subdivision.

What's with all the pebble promos on my driveway?

A pebble promo is a plastic baggie that contains a business card or a folded flyer and a few pebbles. The baggie protects the business card, and the pebbles add weight, enabling the promo to be tossed onto driveways, like a newspaper. Where I live, most of the pebble promos are from landscape maintenance companies. To dispose of a promo, I dump the pebbles in my yard and recycle the business card and the baggie.[*]

What these companies seems to overlook in their marketing strategy is how they're slowly putting themselves out of business by donating pebbles to prospective customers. A pebble-covered yard is drought tolerant, maintenance free, and HOA approved.

Residents mostly ignore pebble promos, so one day, Michael and a few other neighborhood dads walked around the subdivision to pick up a recent round of rocks in baggies. They scattered the promos across the driveway of another dad, Joel, while he was at work. Joel was about to pull into his driveway after work when he saw it littered with pebble promos. He cleaned up the mess and had a good laugh with the other dads.

Months later, on Halloween, Joel handed out candy to most trick-or-treaters but reserved a special treat for certain kids. He dropped a pebble promo into the candy bag of every kid whose dad had pranked him.

––––––

[*]PlasticFilmRecycling.org

How do I protect my front lawn from dog-doo?

Subdivision living can be a tough gig for pets. Dogs need space to run, and cats need to be higher on the food chain. I once had two dogs, but after Big was born, it was time to find them loving homes. In the small backyards of tract houses—some filled with patio furniture, a pool, and a play structure—there's little space for Fido or Fifi to roam, much less to answer the call of nature (unless the home has a side yard).

Most dog owners, where I live, respect the neighborhood houndaries* by walking their dogs in the Common Area. But there are doo dodgers* who ignore what their pets leave behind.

Dog-doo is particularly problematic for the peloton of neighborhood kids whose games of football, soccer, and baseball span several front lawns. Since each lawn is the size of a carpet sample, a single dog-doo triggers an emergency quarantine of the field.

Tracking down a doo dodger takes some detective work. I once sent the peloton on a reconnaissance mission to find out which neighbor had left dog-doo on my lawn. While the kids investigated, I marked the dog-doo with a tomato cage and wrote a short note To Whom It May Concern. The peloton later debriefed me on a list of suspects.

When the prime suspect's dog was seen sniffing around my lawn, the peloton signaled to me. I approached the suspect kindly, pointed to the tomato cage, and explained that this scrap of lawn

---

houndary (*noun*): the boundary where dogs are welcome to pee, poop, play, and explore; typically includes the Common Area and excludes front yards.

doo dodger (*noun*): one who avoids cleaning up after one's pet.

was where the neighborhood kids played. The suspect apologized, which I appreciated, and said she would try to be more mindful of her dog.

As a dog-doo deterrent, I once considered artificial turf. Dogs would, I reasoned, take one sniff of the fake stuff and move on to something familiar, like real grass or a fire hydrant, right?

Wrong.

Dogs seem not to care whether the grass they pee on is fake or real, green or brown, and yet their pee-requisites* seem to be so selective. They stop. They sniff. They sniff over there. They sniff back here. They pause. They sniff again, and *then* they pee. I try to protect my lawn from doo dodgers by staying alert to their three main strategies.

– STRATEGY #1 –

Make the kids walk the dog.

Doo dodgers say that having a pet teaches kids responsibility. No. *Cleaning up* after a pet teaches responsibility. I once spotted a kid letting his dog poop on a neighbor's lawn. When the kid saw me, he yanked on the leash and dragged his dog, mid-poop, back to the sidewalk, leaving a trail of poop pebbles for me to pick up.

– STRATEGY #2 –

Go leash-less.

Arrogant doo dodgers walk Fido without a leash while they read the mail, ride a bike, or stare at their phone. When reminded of leash laws, they proudly announce that Fido is "under voice command." Perhaps. But I've never heard any of them give this simple command: "Fido, don't poop there!"

---

pee-requisites (*plural noun*): the elusive set of pre-conditions that dogs require before they'll tinkle on something.

– STRATEGY #3 –

Walk the dog after dark.

If they can't see it, they can't scoop it. I hope these after-dark doo dodgers step in something else they didn't see: the pile Fido left on last night's walk.

Doo dodgers who ignore basic petiquette* make me want to retaliate. If provoked by poop, I might return the errant dog-doo to its rightful walkway, at dusk, just before the doo dodger's dinner guests arrive.

———

📄 *WHAT THE AD SAYS:*

"A proposed, 35-acre community recreation area with playground, dog park, and aquatic center"

👓 *WHAT IT REALLY MEANS:*

A fantastic amenity has been *proposed* but will remain in pre-construction until new homebuyers have contributed years of property tax and months of Mello-Roos* to fund its construction.

---

petiquette (*noun*): short for *pet etiquette*; the socially acceptable behaviors and choices of pet owners.

Mello-Roos refers to a rather hefty tax attached to tract homes in special districts, for at least 20 years, and used to fund public improvements.

Should I add a tiny house to my backyard?

As Big, Middle, and Little reached their teens, each wanted more independence. I wanted that independence to come with a counterweight of responsibility. I imagined a tiny house, where our teen could learn all about homeownership. The resident of this rookie roost* would pay a pro rata share of the mortgage, property tax, homeowner's insurance, utilities, and the roos and the dues.*

Once our teen had demonstrated the ability to pay his bills on time and care for the rookie roost, the Bank of Mom & Dad might agree to finance an improvement, such as a built-in loft bed, using a rookie roost equity line of credit (RELOC).

Were our teen to default, by spending his RELOC funds on concert tickets or trendy electronics, the Bank of Mom & Dad would foreclose on the rookie roost, and the teen would return to his college-prep bedroom.

———

rookie roost (*noun*): an accessory dwelling unit where a future homeowner can learn about basic repairs, routine maintenance, and regular payments.

roos and the dues, the (*slang*): Mello-Roos and HOA dues.

Does my property have an easement?

During the close of escrow on our Tudor-inspired tract house, I glanced at the property's legal description to be sure there were no easements. Shortly after moving in, I discovered that our driveway included a pleasement.* When the driveway was vacant, neighbors and visitors would use it as they pleased.

Lumbering SUVs would pull in to turn around like ships in a small harbor. Garage sale shoppers would convert it to a loading zone. Youngsters would draw on it with chalk. The peloton would use it as home plate, a skate park, or the finish line for their skid-mark challenge.

My sister once admonished me for a lack of etiquette in regard to a pleasement. I had pulled my squirt hauler into her neighbor's vacant driveway, to turn around. Apparently, I left tire marks on the neighbor's cobblestone upgrade. Proper etiquette, my sister said, is to pull in, back out, and turn my tires only when they're on the street.

Because driveways impact curb appeal and double as venues for happy hours and garage sales, I can understand why people want to protect their concrete or cobblestone. That said, if I want to exact some nonverbal revenge on a nasty neighbor, I know just how to do it!

------

pleasement (*noun*): in a sardine-packed subdivision, the unofficial right of non-owners to use vacant private property, such as a driveway or a front lawn, for their own enjoyment.

4

A Close-knit Community

How can I create community among neighbors?

Tract home builders seem to think that squishing homes together creates a close-knit community. It doesn't. Residents, not builders, are the ones who create community. On my street, residents bond at block parties, happy hours, and garage sales.

From what I've seen, a neighborhood garage sale builds two types of community: wide-area community, when shoppers show up from surrounding subdivisions, and neighborhood community, which is built the night before a garage sale, at the preview party.*

The preview party begins as sellers organize and price their stuff for tomorrow's sale. Non-participating neighbors meander the sidewalk, beverage in hand, and stop at each garage for a sneak peek. That's when the sacred Stuff Sackrament starts to swirl, as neighbors in different life stages buy and sell stuff.

New Parents sell their custom bicycles, designer clothing, and fancy luggage to buy strollers, high chairs, and toys from Parents of School-aged Children. Parents of School-aged Children buy computers and sports equipment from Empty Nesters. Empty Nesters buy sofa beds and home office furniture from Retirees. Retirees buy custom bicycles, designer clothing, and fancy luggage from New Parents, bringing the Stuff Sackrament full circle.

People want their unwanted stuff to go to a good home. The Stuff Sackrament is a communal effort to ensure that the best stuff never leaves the neighborhood.

———

preview party (*noun*): an informal social gathering, held as a progressive event the night before a garage sale, where neighbors participate in the Stuff Sackrament.

Why do *they* live here?

In ads for new subdivisions, the phrase "like-minded neighbors" leaves me shaking my head. How can builders ensure that buyers will be like-minded? In my experience, most neighborhoods have at least one *non*-like-minded neighbor. When I was a kid, that neighbor was The Witch. My friends and I would never trick-or-treat at her house, and if we had to pass it, we'd cross the street.

Where I live now, that neighbor is Mr. Meanie. He drives too fast, he bullies the peloton, and he calls the police to report games of street hockey. He and Mrs. Meanie appear to dislike kids, but they bought a four-bedroom house that backs up to a large, public high school, making me wonder, *Why do* they *live here?*

But non-like-minded neighbors can also bring authenticity and depth to the shallow image of the ideal neighborhood. Who better to help refine the virtues of patience and tolerance? Who better to provide resistance for kids to push against as they mature? Adults who are irrational and unpredictable sometimes strengthen neighborhoods and create community by giving other residents a crisis to rally around or a story to laugh about.

————

Where did all the flags go?

Flags are what first led me to Avocado Village. Flags once pointed the way to shiny new tract homes in North City West. Subdivision builders mark streets, sales offices, and model tours with flags. Yet, the homes they sell never come with a flag, a flagpole, or even a flag bracket. After builders sell the homes in a subdivision, they pull up their flags and leave.

But flags find their way back.

Residents in subdivisions fly national flags, state flags, and team flags. They fly seasonal flags for Valentine's Day, St. Patrick's Day, Spring, Halloween, and Thanksgiving. Every house looks better with a flag, and in the dirt yard surrounding a new tract house, a flagpole can double as a tree-quivalent.* Natural trees require maintenance and take years to grow. A tree-quivalent can be put up in a day.

More Than Décor

Flags are more than décor. The very first status update wasn't on Facebook. It was on a flagpole. If I want to "post" about Middle's Little League team doing well, I can fly a baseball-icon flag at full staff. Flying it at half-staff would signal to fans that the team is in a state of distress. Maybe they're on a losing streak, or they performed poorly in a weekend tournament.

Flying a Thanksgiving flag at full staff would let my neighbors know that dinner is proceeding smoothly. Flying it at half-staff

---

tree-quivalent (*noun*): a tall, fabricated object that functions visually like a tree but requires little or no maintenance, such as a flagpole, a lamp post, an owl box, or a freestanding basketball hoop.

would indicate petty conflicts. Flying a white flag below a Thanksgiving flag would indicate that, while the situation is tense, a truce has been reached.

With a flagpole, I could provide immediate, nonverbal feedback to contractors working on my house. Hoisting a contractor's lawn sign to full staff would let the crew (and my neighbors) know that I'm satisfied with the quality of work. Lowering the sign to half-staff would imply that there's room for improvement. Instead of awkward conversations or one-star reviews, I could just point to the flagpole.

All Upgrades Completed

If we ever decide to move, I may search online for a house and use *flagpole* as a keyword. Why? Because installing a flagpole is never a top priority. A homeowner who found time to install a flagpole has obviously completed all other upgrades.

———

 *WHAT THE AD SAYS:*

"The natural choice for home and habitat"

WHAT IT REALLY MEANS:

It *was* the natural choice for habitat, until a builder chose it for homes.

How do I spot the former models in my subdivision?

Flags and model homes go together like chips and guacamole, but in a subdivision where the flags are long gone, how do I spot the former model homes? Two words: original owners. Residents who purchase their home directly from the builder are the unofficial historians of the 'hood.

I consulted one of these historians when, on a walk around the block, I saw a garage that didn't match the others. The garage door had air vents running across the top and bottom, as if something inside needed to breathe. To the right of the garage was a tiny room with a window. When the window blind was up, I could see a sink and a toilet. Down the left side of the garage were more windows with blinds. The house next door had its own oddity: a concrete walkway that ended abruptly in the middle of the lawn. It looked like the contractor left to get more concrete and never came back.

I asked an original owner, and he told me these houses had been two of the four models for our subdivision. He pointed out the other two and said the cutoff walkway had been part of the model tour. The vented garage had been the sales office.

———

📄 *WHAT THE AD SAYS:*

"Private compartmented water closet"

✍ *WHAT IT REALLY MEANS:*

The toilet has its own room.

How did my floor-plan friend solve this?

We were renting a custom house when four-year-old Big had a new friend over for a playdate. In the middle of playtime, New Friend ran into my kitchen in a panic. He needed a bathroom—fast! I pointed toward the hallway and said, "Go to the hallway, turn right, and it's the first door on your right." But my directions were too complicated, and seconds later, New Friend peed all over my kitchen floor.

Since moving to a cookie-cutter home, zero friends have peed on my floor. When a new friend asks where the bathroom is, the peloton says, "It's just like at Jason's house." If the new friend hasn't been to Jason's house, the kids rattle off other names until the friend recognizes a floor plan.

When I meet a neighbor who has my same floor plan, I feel an instant connection, as if we share similar tastes and deal with similar problems. Subdivision kids sometimes make a best floor-plan friend. BFFs occupy the same bedroom in the same floor plan.

In my two-story home, the kitchen and master bathroom are located as far away as possible from the water heater. Hot water takes two minutes to arrive at the kitchen sink and longer to arrive at the master bathroom upstairs. Fortunately, one of my floor-plan friends figured out a fix and let me in on her secret: She starts the dishwasher before she showers, so the hot water arrives faster.

———

How do I copy a neighbor's upgrade?

Builders, with their richly decorated model homes, want to remind me that, given unlimited funds, even a tract house could qualify for a Pottery Barn photo shoot. Until those funds arrive, I'll continue to rely on my neighbors' houses for budget-friendly upgrade ideas.

My subdivision has four floor plans spread across 188 homes. That gives me forty-seven dioramas of the dos and don'ts for my Plan 3. Some residents in cookie-cutter communities dislike being copied, so there's an art to it. I use one strategy to copy curbside upgrades and another for backyard or interior upgrades.

Curbside Upgrades

To copy a curbside upgrade, like a paint scheme, a landscape layout, or a front-yard water feature, I look for an inspiration home that's outside the visual vicinity of my home. Residents upgrade their exteriors, in part, to remind themselves which house is theirs. If I copy an exterior improvement from a home very near to mine, those residents might walk in my front door by mistake.

Once I've selected an inspiration home, I then find a way to introduce myself to the resident. If I'm feeling extroverted, I might walk or drive past the inspiration home at various times of the day, hoping to spot the resident outdoors, where I can casually strike up a conversation. If I'm feeling introverted, I might ask another neighbor to introduce me.

When I'm face to face with the resident, I introduce myself, compliment the improvement, and then ask respectfully where I might find something similar. I disclose my street address early in the interaction, to indicate that my home is comfortably outside the visual vicinity of the inspiration home.

My candor, however, doesn't obligate a resident to reciprocate with equal candor. Residents who suspect they're being copied have no moral obligation to disclose their sources or to answer truthfully. That's an outcome I have to consider when skimming for design ideas.

Backyard and Interior Upgrades

If I want to copy a backyard or an interior upgrade, I have three options in each category.

Backyard Upgrades

To copy, say, a patio cover, a built-in barbecue, or a chicken coop, I first have to find an inspiration yard. Using Google Maps to peer into nearby yards is a good first step, but it doesn't supply enough detail. I need to inspect workmanship, size, and color. I need to ask questions about cost and completion time.

Gaining access to the backyards of neighbors who know me is relatively easy. In general, they're happy to show off their upgrade. But I'm a shopper who makes her decision only after she's seen *everything*, so I want to visit as many inspiration yards as I can.

– OPTION #1 –
Air Surveillance

I can pick an inspiration yard using Google Maps, position one of my kids on the sidewalk nearby, and then hand over the controller for a drone. When the drone disappears into the inspiration yard, I can accompany my pilot to knock on the resident's front door and hope for an invitation to the crash site, where I can take a closer look at the upgrade.

– OPTION #2 –

Small Animal on the Loose

I can send a small animal over the fence of various inspiration yards, knock on the front door, and ask to retrieve my pet.

– OPTION #3 –

Tree House or Trampoline

Visual vicinity isn't a factor when copying backyard upgrades, so I can set up a tree house or a trampoline in my yard and then aim a telephoto lens at inspiration yards to generate images for my vision board.

Interior Upgrades

To copy an interior upgrade, such as flooring, a wall treatment, or a kitchen remodel, Google Maps is no help at all, but sites like Zillow, Redfin, and Trulia can provide close-up views if a home has recently been listed for sale or rent.

If my inspiration home isn't on one of these sites, I have to find a way to gain access as an invited guest. With neighbors who know me, I can ask outright to see their upgrade, but neighbors I don't know need more of a nudge. Three options are open to me.

– OPTION #1 –

Talk to the contractors.

I can strike up a conversation with the contractors when they're on a break or fetching tools from their truck. Ideally, they'll invite me into the house to show off their work.

– OPTION #2 –

View when vacant.

If the house is a rental, I can peek through the windows when it's vacant.

– Option #3 –

Be an adult.

Let's say that my neighbor, Stella, mentions that Harriet and Roger are remodeling their kitchen. I can ask Stella to introduce me to Harriet and Roger. Or, if Harriet and Roger have my same floor plan, this offers a social segue in cookie-cutter culture where I can introduce myself directly, to ask for floor-plan advice.

The direct approach carries two risks. The first is that Harriet and Roger might be mid-makeover.* If that's the case, my visit won't yield as much detailed information as if I were to wait until their remodel is complete.

The second risk is that Harriet and Roger might covet their coveted residence so deeply that they want to protect their sources. They do this by telling little white lies. If I knock on Harriet and Roger's front door, here's what might be said:

"Hi, I'm Julie. I live down the street in the same floor plan. Are you Harriet?"

"Yes," says Harriet. "It's nice to meet you. I think our kids have played together."

"I think they have," I say and smile. "My husband and I have talked about redoing our kitchen, and Stella said you did a fabulous job on yours."

"Oh, do you want to come in and see it?" asks Harriet.

I step inside and immediately notice a beautiful silver-framed mirror in the foyer. I follow Harriet to the kitchen. "Oh wow, this countertop is stunning," I say, running my hand over the smooth stone. "Where did you find this quartz?"

Now, while Harriet may have happily shown off her updated kitchen to Stella, because she and Stella have different floor plans, Harriet may not be as forthcoming with me because she and I could end up with identical kitchens.

---

mid-makeover (*adjective*): the state of being in the middle of a home remodeling project.

"Hmm," Harriet says. "I'm not sure. We may have bought it at a place that was going out of business." I smell a lie-pology.* Harriet forgetting where she recently spent thousands of dollars is a sign that she's uninterested in sharing her source. So, I move on to a different subject.

"The wall color you chose goes so well with the floor. Is that real wood or a laminate?" I ask.

"Oh, my husband picked out the floor," Harriet says with a sigh. "It's probably a laminate from Ikea. He's too cheap to buy the real stuff."

An answer like this can also signal deception. Being so quick to share a source with a stranger and mentioning how inexpensive the product was can mean Harriet is protecting her real source by offering a cheap imposter. This ploy is intended to send a naive copycat on a wild goose chase through Ikea's flooring department, looking for something that doesn't exist. I'm a veteran copycat, so I'll verify Harriet's answers with some online research.

I admire the kitchen a little longer, take copious mental notes, and then head to the foyer. My visit is brief since Harriet is clearly a coveter. As I reach for the front door, I pause and say, "This mirror is gorgeous. Where did you find it?"

"Oh that? It was passed down from my husband's side of the family."

"Huh," I say and then attempt to call Harriet's bluff. "It looks so much like a mirror I saw at Costco recently."

Harriet wrings her hands like an ulterior designer* who has nearly blown her cover. Then she says, "Oh, you know what? You're right. I did buy this one at Costco. The mirror in the living room is the heirloom piece."

---

lie-pology (*noun*): a fib combined with an apology.

ulterior designer (*noun*): a subdivision resident who lies about or conceals the source of furniture, flooring, décor, and the like, with the hope of having a unique home.

When it looks as if I might be rushing out the door and heading to Costco, Harriet adds, "But it could be a Costco collectible* by now."

Touché! While I've mastered the art of copycatting, Harriet has mastered the art of ulterior design.

———

 WHAT THE AD SAYS:

"Pot drawers"

WHAT IT REALLY MEANS:

The kitchen has oversized drawers for storing cookware or marijuana.

Costco collectible (*proper noun*): an item once purchased at Costco but never available again.

Do I need a permit?

After we moved to Washington State for Michael's job, we bought a tract house built in 1978, with the mauve toilets to prove it. One spring day, we had the rickety aluminum windows replaced with double-pane, vinyl windows. This energy-saving upgrade qualified for reimbursement from the local utility company, but filing the proper paperwork had delayed the installation date.

The day after the project was finally finished, I found myself sitting by a sunny window, happy to be looking *out* the window instead of *at* the window. Then my landline rang.

"Hello?" I said.

"Hi, this is Bob Roy from the building inspector's office. Am I speaking to the homeowner?"

"Yes," I said.

"My files indicate that you recently installed new windows in your home. Is that correct?"

"Yes," I said, more cautiously.

"Well, I don't see a window permit in my file. Did you secure one before the installation?"

"A window permit? No, I didn't know I needed one." My breathing grew shallow. I'd heard scary stories about permits and building inspectors.

"Well yes, you should have secured a permit before any work was done. Are the windows installed?" he asked.

"Yes," I said, holding my breath for what was coming.

"Okay then, let me grab my calendar. I'll need to set up a time for one of our guys to come out there and inspect the openings."

"Inspect the openings?" I asked.

"Yeah, what he'll do is pull out each window, inspect the opening to make sure it's up to code, and then reinstall the window—at your expense, of course."

Oh my gosh!! I was shaking now. I didn't want any trouble with the building inspector, but Michael and I had no money to pay for an inspection, a reinstallation, or a permit. I started to cry.

"You're kidding, right?" I squeaked.

"No ma'am. Window permits are standard in any window replacement job. It's for the safety of the homeowner. Now, do you have your calendar?" he asked.

I reached for my calendar. "I really wish you were kidding. I don't know how I'm gonna afford this."

"Actually ma'am, I am kidding. April Fools' from your neighbor, Lisa." I didn't speak to Lisa for a month.

Like me, there are other subdivision residents who know next to nothing about building codes, permits, and CC&Rs. Pranksters or people taking a power trip* will sometimes impersonate local authorities and pretend to cite neighbors for various infractions. They'll send a formally worded letter, make a phone call, or slap a fake Notice of Non-compliance on the front door for "violations" like these:

- Failing to secure advance approval for an exterior upgrade, such as a paint scheme, landscape, or hardscape.

- Detracting from neighborhood neutrality with flashy window coverings, decorative house numbers, or a unique mailbox.

- Parking unacceptable vehicles on the street.

- Setting out trash cans at the curb too early.

---

power trip (*noun*): a free or low-cost vacation alternative.

- Appearing to have abandoned a property, as evidenced by a neglected yard or a driveway littered with faded flyers, old newspapers, or pebble promos.

- Creating a nuisance (e.g., noises, odors, pets).

- Under-decorating a home's curbside exterior during the holiday season, also known as being ornamentally challenged.*

📄 *WHAT THE AD SAYS:*

"Home exteriors evoking Cottage, European Cottage, or Rustic Cottage architecture"

👓 *WHAT IT REALLY MEANS:*

Home exteriors that differ about as much as vanilla, vanilla bean, and old-fashioned vanilla ice cream.

---

ornamentally challenged (*adjective*): a seasonal decorative disorder marked by the inability to acceptably decorate the curbside exterior of one's home, especially during the winter holidays. (*Thank you to Jim B. for this gem.*)

How can I offset the cost of an upgrade?

A neighbor of mine once had a rustic willow armchair adorning her front porch. When I asked where she bought it, she didn't bother fibbing. She said simply, "I'm not gonna tell you because then you'll go get one like it, and mine will no longer be unique." I listened as she lamented over an earlier incident with copycats. She had painted her house, and soon afterward, two neighbors within visual vicinity painted their houses in a similar color.

In the months that followed, I started to notice the phenomenon that my neighbor had described. It occurred so often that I called this corollary the Rule of Three, which states,

> If one resident does it,
> two neighbors will also do it.

If one resident buys a new garage door, two neighbors will also buy new garage doors. If one resident replaces a fence, two neighbors will also replace their fences.

After Michael and I had the windows replaced on our Tudor-inspired house, the contractor handed me a short stack of business cards and said, "We pay fifty bucks for each referral." I realized the Rule of Three could help offset the cost of our upgrade. I set the cards by my front door and handed them out as copycats came calling. Within a few months, two referral bonuses showed up.

Being the first to upgrade puts me in the best position for referral bonuses, but it can be more costly than being a copycat. That's because a contractor's learning curve is steepest on the first house. If I'm the copycat, I benefit from less guesswork, which can mean lower costs and shorter completion times. Plus, having seen the finished result on the first neighbor's house, I can make informed decisions about project details. It's like having a model of a remodel.

———

 *WHAT THE AD SAYS:*

"2-bay garage"

WHAT IT REALLY MEANS:

Covered parking for two compact cars, one mid-sized sedan, or the front half of a premium SUV.

What can neighbors do about a vacant house in foreclosure?

Upgrading is a core value of cookie-cutter culture. People in subdivisions enjoy upgrading homes, cars, and hotel accommodations. I went to one Open House where the owners—I'll call them the Joneses—had taken upgrading to an extreme.

They'd remodeled a tract house with recessed lighting, crown molding, wallpaper, wood-framed windows, high-end fixtures, and commercial-grade appliances. The floors, however, remained in their original, late '80s condition: worn-out wood parquet in the dining room, chipped builder-grade tile with brown grout in the kitchen, stained white carpet in the living room. It appeared the Joneses had run out of money before upgrading the last item on their list: the floors. They needed to sell the house because they were probably facing floorclosure.*

Floorclosure and foreclosure lead to the same financial cliff, but people like the Joneses seem to take a running start when they prioritize home improvement over homeownership. That's like buying an expensive stereo for a rental car.

Yes, it's sad to lose neighbors to foreclosure, but what if the bank-owned beauty they left behind were morphed into a subdivision clubhouse? The home likely has a pool, a hot tub, and a built-in barbecue. What a shame to let such amenities go to waste while the home awaits a short sale.

---

floorclosure (*noun*): being unable to pay the mortgage after overspending on upgrades; characterized by a house where everything has been upgraded except the floors.

Any homeowner who weathered the Great Recession knows that a vacant, lifeless house can drag down the values of nearby houses. Throwing no-host parties in the Joneses' old place could make it look occupied, keep values from tanking, and reduce the wear and tear from hosted parties held in individual homes.

Could the Joneses' gourmet kitchen island workstation be used for cooking classes? Could the neighborhood kids have birthday parties in the backyard pool? Personally, I'd love a local gym. That three-car garage probably has an epoxy-coated floor and melamine cabinets, making it the perfect spot for neighbors to consolidate their home gym equipment. No more excuses for not working out. The gym is within walking distance.

 **WHAT THE AD SAYS:**

"Luxurious flooring with striking base moldings"

WHAT IT REALLY MEANS:

Two-inch moldings for when the vacuum cleaner strikes the baseboard.

Is it better to buy or lease a car?

In a small town, everyone knows everyone else's business. In a *sprawl* town, everyone knows everyone else's cars. Master-planned communities are designed around convenient car travel, so I cross paths with friends and acquaintances in parking lots, at intersections, and in the school valet lane. The ability to quickly recognize a car lets me be the first to wave or the first to look away.

At a sports facility or a playing field, a familiar car in the parking lot acts as a beacon for arriving teammates. "Hey, there's Eli's dad's car, so this must be the right place."

On the other hand, when I see an unfamiliar car parked on my street, I'm immediately suspicious. *Who's parked in front of Jerry and Jeri's house?* Usually, it's a leased car.

I wave to car owners more often than I wave to people who lease cars, for the simple reason that owners drive the same car year after year, making it easy for me to peg them to a particular car. Drivers who lease cars have to put in extra effort to remind neighbors, like me, which car is theirs. They can do this by driving the carpool more often, parking in their driveway consistently, or washing the car in front of their house.

If a leased car has window tint on the driver's side, it takes me about three years to recognize the car quickly enough to wave. Without tint, about two years. Unfortunately, two to three years is also the length of the average car lease. Just when I start to wave regularly, the driver leases a new car, and the recognition factor reverts to zero.

———

Should I wave to anyone who waves at me?

One afternoon, driving home from work, Michael found himself following a white squirt hauler and assumed it was mine. He was sure of it when the squirt hauler turned onto our street and pulled into a driveway. Michael parked his car at the curb and stepped out to kiss his wife. Except, the woman who stepped out of the squirt hauler wasn't his wife, and that's when Michael noticed this wasn't his house. He'd parked at Paula's house.

Paula and I drive identical squirt haulers, and our hair color is the same, so we're occasionally mistaken for each other. To avoid offending any of Paula's friends who might mistake me for her, I wave to anyone who waves at me, even if that person is my own husband waving at "Paula."

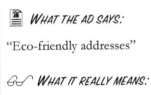

WHAT THE AD SAYS:

"Eco-friendly addresses"

WHAT IT REALLY MEANS:

House numbers that fall off and biodegrade long before the house does.

Is there a way to slow down the speeding cars on my street?

We live so close to a high school that drivers use our street as a shortcut to the student parking lot. Nine months a year, our street sounds like a mini Indy 500 in the morning, at lunch, and after school. Neighbors have tried waving their arms and shouting, but the drama does nothing to slow down the speeders.

One day, I saw Paula's seventh grader crouched in between two cars parked at the curb. He was holding a clipboard, so I asked what he was doing. He told me he was collecting data for a math assignment on means and averages. As a speeding car approached, he would stand up, point a radar gun, and record the car's speed. Drivers who saw the gun slowed down immediately.

I don't own a radar gun, and renting one is pretty expensive. But I do own something that resembles a radar gun, especially at 45 miles per hour. Now, if I need to remind drivers about speed limits, I can crouch behind a parked car, pop up, and pretend to clock their speed on my blow dryer.

———

How do I deal with noise in my subdivision?

In a close-knit community, noise must be managed. I deal with the cacophony of barking, shouting, drumming, strumming, revving, mowing, and blowing by allocating imaginary noise credits to households within earshot of mine. Like pollution credits issued by the U.S. Environmental Protection Agency, noise credits are based on the average amount of noise generated by a typical household. Unlike pollution credits, noise credits can't be bought, sold, or bartered because no one knows they exist.

Noise credits represent the amount of social or personal ruckus I'm willing to tolerate over a given time period. Social ruckus comes from backyard barbecues, karaoke machines, and dinner parties where the drinking gets out of hand. Personal ruckus comes from pets, yard care, construction, and arguments. If someone in the household plays the tuba, the drums, or the cello, I add extra credits to cover practice time. Noise credits don't apply on New Year's Eve or July 4th. My guess is that other people issue imaginary noise credits because I've noticed party hosts using three methods to conserve theirs.

– METHOD #1 –
Invite a loud neighbor to your noise event.

In my subdivision, where houses stand ten feet apart, it's tempting to blame the *loudest* noise for *all* the noise. For example, if Dave hosts a backyard barbecue, he might invite Gary, the neighbor with the raucous laugh. When Gary's laugh is the loudest noise coming from Dave's barbecue, non-invited neighbors are likely to deduct noise credits from Gary's account, not Dave's.

– METHOD #2 –

Notify non-invited neighbors in advance.

One day, I opened my front door and sitting on the doormat was a clear plastic bakery box holding a humongous slice of cheesecake topped with strawberries. The attached note was from my next-door neighbor. She would be hosting a thirtieth-birthday bash this weekend and had rented a karaoke machine. I reciprocated with a rich helping of extra noise credits.

– METHOD #3 –

Offer ultra-sensitive neighbors a night away.

I've heard of hosts who offer ultra-sensitive neighbors a free or discounted hotel room for the night of the noise event.

How do I spot the noisemakers in a neighborhood? First, I look to the Plan 4 homes. The terms *Plan 4* and *the Party Plan* are slang for the largest floor plan in a subdivision. Simple math says a larger house can hold more people, so it's likely to emit more noise. I also look for lifestyle enhancements. Homeowners with a lot of equity will sometimes borrow that equity to pay for home upgrades, luxury cars, or elaborate trips. The more money people spend to enhance their lifestyle, the more they want to talk about it. And that creates noise.

———

How can I squelch background noise in a home office?

When I'm on a phone call, the background noise on the other end tells me whether that person is working from an on-site office, a home office, or the checkout line at the grocery store. Each has a unique noise profile.

On-site Office

- Fingers tapping computer keys
- Phones chirping with alerts
- Printers churning out paper
- Muffled conversations between co-workers

Home Office

- Screaming or barking
- Running water
- Trash truck
- Garage band
- Leaf blower
- Music from ice cream truck

Grocery Store

- Scanner beeps
- Price check requests
- Muzak

I've had my home office in a dining area, a bedroom, and a walk-in closet under the stairs. Twice, background noise has driven me to rent space in an office building. There, I heard new types of unpleasant noises: street crews using jackhammers, toilets flushing on the other side of my wall, and tenants leaving their door open during meetings and conference calls. I returned to the familiar noise profile of my home office and established two methods for dealing with noise.

– Method #1 –
The Lie-pology

I learned this method from a woman whose home office was in a garage on an alley. If she was on a business call when a delivery truck roared past or the trash truck was collecting, she would say, "Sorry about the noise. We're expanding our offices." If I'm on a business call when my toddler stands under the vaulted ceiling and shouts, "I GO POTTY RIGHT NOW!," I might use a lie-pology and say, "Sorry for the interruption. It's Take Your Daughters and Sons to Work Day."

– Method #2 –
The Audio Recoat

In the home improvement industry, recoating is a process used to cover unsightly surfaces, such as garage floors, countertops, and bathtubs. My current office is a backyard shed, so I use an audio recoat to cover most types of background noise. For a soothing white-noise recoat during phone calls or video meetings, I turn on a fan. To block out the neighbor's pool guy chatting on his phone, I play instrumental music.

I also deal with serious background noise from gas-powered lawn mowers, trimmers, and leaf blowers. Professional gardeners go from house to house six days a week in my subdivision, whipping up ten-minute tornadoes of rage-inducing noise and toxic air.

My puny white-noise recoat is no match for the 80 decibels coming off these macho grass-and-leaf slayers nor can my portable air conditioner filter exhaust fumes spewed by two-stroke engines. When gardeners fire up their equipment, I shut my windows, put on headphones, and go to OneSquareInch.org to flood my ears with soundtracks of natural silence from Olympic National Park's Hoh Rain Forest.

———

 WHAT THE AD SAYS:

"Decorative model background music"

WHAT IT REALLY MEANS:

Each floor plan has a playlist.

Do I notify noisy neighbors or align my noise to theirs?

If a neighboring household whips through its noise credits, I'm left with two options: sending a note or aligning my noise to theirs.

The Anonymous Note

To deal with a barking dog, I might send a note like this one:

> *Dear Neighbor,*
>
> *We're writing out of concern for your puppy. Although you may not realize it, your pup has recently been barking for hours at a time. Presumably, no one is home to let the pup indoors.*
>
> *While the pup's health and safety are our main concerns, we also worry that a less tolerant neighbor might contact Animal Control to have the pup removed.*
>
> *Sincerely,*
> *Your neighbors*

I use the word *puppy* even if the dog is a full-grown nuisance. Typing the note is faster, but a handwritten note is more personal, especially a note adorned with those wildlife stickers that come in the mail. Video doorbells, like Ring, make it impossible to hand deliver an anonymous note, but I can hire the peloton to deliver it and pay them in Popsicles.

Noise Alignment

My other option is to align my ruckus with the neighbors' ruckus. I do this by generating noise that harmonizes with their noise.

Theirs: Barking dog
Mine: Chopping firewood or using a hammer

Theirs: Chainsaw, wood chipper, or stump grinder
Mine: Circular saw, sander, or vacuum cleaner

Theirs: Pressure washer
Mine: Hose on "jet" setting to clean 400-gallon rain barrel

Theirs: Pool party
Mine: Gushing water while refilling rain barrel

Odor Alignment

Odor alignment works in the same way.

Theirs: Cigarette or cigar smoke
Mine: Spray paint

Theirs: Chlorine from pool maintenance
Mine: Open bags of composted chicken manure

 *WHAT THE AD SAYS:*

"Hushed flooring"

WHAT IT REALLY MEANS:

The laminate floor has underlayment, like every laminate floor ever installed.

5

CONVENIENT SHOPPING

How do I discourage door-to-door solicitors?

The *most* convenient shopping is shopping from home, but not from door-to-door solicitors. I've opened my front door to people selling pest control, cleaning products, religion, magazines, and meat. Solicitors use a variety of tactics, and over the years, I've tailored a response to the most common tactics.

– RESPONSE #1 –

What a coincidence!

Solicitors in their twenties will sometimes introduce themselves as kids from the neighborhood. Here's how I dealt with Tad after he knocked on my front door.

"Hey, how's it goin'? I'm Tad—you know, Dolores and Ken's son from down the street?"

I shook my head. "I've lived here twelve years Tad, and I don't know anyone named Dolores or Ken."

"Right, okay. So look, I *really* need your help. If you buy just twenty-five dollars of magazine subscriptions, it would *really* help me out because then I'll be able to go to Hawaii with my soccer team, and I *really* want to go to Hawaii."

"What a coincidence, Tad! I *really* want to go to Hawaii, too. I'm saving up for my own trip, so I can't help with yours. Aloha!" Then I smiled and closed the door.

- RESPONSE #2 -

Unfriend the too friendly.

Some solicitors try to forge a front-door friendship, as if their sales manager said, "Be friendly. People like to buy from their friends." Maybe. But I've never heard anyone say, "I met my buddy Nate when he stopped by my house selling microfiber cleaning cloths."

Solicitors who want to be my friend will open their pitch with something like, "Hi! How's your day goin' so far?"

To which I reply, "It's busy."

"Fantastic! Hey, so my name is Josh, and you are … ?"

"Not interested." Then I smile and close the door.

- RESPONSE #3 -

Members only.

Above my doorbell is a sign that enables callers to sort themselves.

Please …

UPS, FedEx, HGTV,
Trick-or-Treaters & Scouts only.

No solicitors, charity workers,
or those on religious missions.

Thank you!

If a solicitor ignores the sign and rings my doorbell, I open the door, point to the sign, and shrug, as if the house came with the sign, and there's nothing I can do about it.

- RESPONSE #4 -

A Previous Engagement

I open the front door and stand there holding a toilet plunger.

– RESPONSE #5 –

The Blanket Statement

If a solicitor won't shut up, I interrupt with a statement that covers all products and services: "Sorry, I'm a penniless, agnostic, illiterate vegan who doesn't clean."

– RESPONSE #6 –

A Controlled Area

Occasionally, an unmarked van will drop off a group of solicitors to canvas my street. If I see more than one person strolling the sidewalk with a lanyard and a badge, I might declare a front-porch pandemic by sticking a controlled-area label on my door, like one of these:

- QUARANTINE
- DANGER
- BIOHAZARD

– RESPONSE #7 –

Baby sleeping.

There's one more type of door-to-door caller I want to discourage, but these people aren't solicitors. They're the buyers who ring my doorbell at 6 a.m. on garage sale day to ask if I have any jewelry or electronics for sale. I tried ignoring them, but they were relentless. What finally worked was this sign taped on my front door: *Do not disturb. Baby sleeping.*

———

Why do some drivers park at colored curbs?

At shopping malls in my master-planned community, most drivers park in marked stalls, but I was curious about the subset of drivers who park at colored curbs. Then, the U.S. Department of Homeland Security stepped in and solved the mystery with its color-coded terror alert system. The colors correlate perfectly to what I see at the mall: self-selected drivers parked at convenience curbs.*

The Red Curb

The red curb is designated for drivers in a SEVERE hurry, such as firefighters, paramedics, or luxury car owners in the throes of a me-mergency.*

The Yellow Curb

The yellow curb attracts drivers whose pace is ELEVATED. They're too hurried to find a marked stall but not hurried enough to park in a fire lane.

The Blue Curb

Drivers who park at the blue curb, without displaying the International Symbol of Access, are GUARDED about how busy they are and whether or not they're parked illegally.

---

convenience curb (*noun*): a red, yellow, blue, or green street curb used by drivers who believe they are too busy to park in marked stalls.

me-mergency (*noun*): a subjective measure of severity.

The Green Curb

Drivers parked at the green curb face a LOW risk of receiving a citation since officers are too busy ticketing drivers at red, yellow, and blue curbs.

Amazon Prime Parking

Does Amazon Prime include prime parking? I see unmarked vans parked and double-parked at convenience curbs, on sidewalks, and blocking driveways. My squirt hauler happens to be an unmarked van. Do I just order an orange traffic vest on Amazon, toss the empty box on my dashboard, and then park wherever I want to?

 *WHAT THE AD SAYS:*

"RV-sized lots"

WHAT IT REALLY MEANS:

Space for a second home and a side income from an RVRBO.

When can teens shop at the mall without an adult?

Major world cultures have rites of passage for teenagers entering adulthood, and cookie-cutter culture has one, too: shopping. From an early age, subdivision kids ride in shopping carts, steer toy cars attached to shopping carts, or push mini shopping carts, like ducklings, behind Mom or Dad. As my kids reached their teens, they wanted to spread their wings and shop without adult supervision.

When Big turned sixteen, I learned that student drivers here in California are allowed to have friends in the car only after a driver has fulfilled a set of graduated license requirements. These requirements, I realized, could be adapted to emancipating teen shoppers. Careless shopping is the number one cause of debt among teens, and distracted teens are dangerous spenders.

GRADUATED SHOPPING REQUIREMENTS

Student shoppers must complete at least 50 hours of practice shopping with a parent or another shopper age 25 or older. Of these practice hours, 10 must be spent night shopping, and 10 must be spent grocery shopping. Practice time provides teen shoppers with a working knowledge of store etiquette, dressing room behavior, payment methods, and return policies.

Student shoppers must complete a six-month period of supervised shopping, where an adult remains twenty paces behind the student shopper but is still able to take control of the credit card, if necessary.

Student shoppers must maintain a clean shopping record, free of shoplifting violations, damage claims, or being banned from stores.

Student shoppers must obey all restrictions on shopping curfews during the twelve-month provisional period after the student shopper is permitted to shop independently.

Student shoppers must obey all restrictions on shopping with other student shoppers.

Student shoppers must carry a fully charged phone in order to remain in contact with a supervising adult during independent shopping trips. Student shoppers must respond to all phone calls or texts immediately. No charge on the cell phone means no charging at the mall.

———

 *WHAT THE AD SAYS:*

"Harmonious floor plans"

WHAT IT REALLY MEANS:

No interior doors and nothing but load-bearing walls. With no doors to slam or walls to hide behind, this floor plan forces family harmony.

Why are Target and Home Depot always near each other?

When I drive along the parkways that connect large subdivisions or master-planned communities, the scenery repeats itself. I pass welcome walls, then shopping malls, then welcome walls, then shopping malls, then more walls, then more malls.

What also repeats is the collection of stores. Certain retailers seem to team up. For example, if I see a Target store, I know there's a Home Depot nearby. I've memorized these four combos:

- Target and Home Depot
- Marshalls and Ross
- Barnes & Noble and Starbucks
- Subway and a gas station

What's the point of memorizing these? If I'm lost, it's faster to figure out where I am by using the monstrous letters on a mall sign than by squinting at a microscopic map on my phone.

––––––

 *WHAT THE AD SAYS:*

"Memorable exteriors"

WHAT IT REALLY MEANS:

What you'll remember most is how they all look alike.

What has Costco done to my supply sensor?

Even when a new subdivision sits in the middle of nowhere, the builder will advertise it as being "close to all," if there's a Costco nearby. A single Costco location offers products in every category and a strip mall of services: a gas station, a tire center, a pharmacy, a hearing and vision clinic, and a photo counter. For me, the only real inconvenience of joining Costco has been the recalibration of my supply sensor.*

As a college student, my supply sensor was set so low that I'd write *toilet paper* on my shopping list when I was down to one roll. After I married and became a mom, my sensor shifted upward to where I'd write *toilet paper* on the shopping list when my family was down to one four-pack.

Joining Costco launched my supply sensor to the stratosphere, causing me to now write *toilet paper* on the shopping list when my household is down to its last thirty rolls.

———

📰 *WHAT THE AD SAYS:*

"Planned retail"

✍️ *WHAT IT REALLY MEANS:*

No retail.

———

supply sensor (*noun*): an internal alert that, when triggered, causes one to add an item to one's shopping list.

6

Youth Sports

How many snacks should I bring for the team?

I've witnessed a dramatic shift in halftime and post-game snacks. In the mid-1990s, the designated snack family* was asked to bring a jug of water and some sliced oranges. A few years later, I noticed that snack families were competing off the field just as fiercely as their players were on the field. Sliced oranges and water had been replaced with energy bars, baked goods, and shimmering bottles of red-, white-, and blue-flavored* sports drinks.

One tradition that hasn't changed is the post-game ritual of players belting out a quick cheer for their opponents. Where losing teams had once sulked as they left the field, now all players run (faster than they ever ran during the game) to their respective snack camps.* There, young athletes load up on cookies, muffins, cupcakes, donuts, and candy. Snack time has become the third half, the fifth quarter, and the tenth inning.

And who else shows up at snack camp? Everyone. I've seen siblings, parents, grandparents, friends, and visiting relatives help themselves to team snacks. I ran out of snacks several times before I figured out that, in cookie-cutter culture, snack time isn't about

---

snack family (*noun*): a team member's immediate relatives who are assigned to bring a smorgasbord of halftime and post-game goodies to a youth sports game.

-flavored (*suffix*): a term combined with a color name to specify one's choice of sports drink: *Mom, can you get me red-flavored Gatorade at the snack bar?*

snack camp (*noun*): a picnic blanket, wagon, or collapsible table from which a snack family serves halftime and post-game snacks to participants at a youth sports game.

refueling. It's about rewarding. Snacks and participation trophies[*]
seem to follow the same philosophy:

Reward participation,
not performance.

Fans who show up at snack camp probably view themselves as
participants, for cheering during the game, and therefore deserving
of a reward.

———

📋 *WHAT THE AD SAYS:*

"Beautiful quartz countertops, upgraded cabinets, and
high-arc kitchen faucet to make all your cooking dreams
come true!"

〰️ *WHAT IT REALLY MEANS:*

Good luck cooking without a stove.

———

participation trophy (*noun*): a trinket given to every player on a team,
regardless of the team's win-loss record.

How much should I budget for team sports?

When Big was eight, Michael coached his soccer team. As a thank-you gift to Michael, the team parent had the players sign a soccer ball with their name and number. It was a simple gift that Michael cherished, especially because one player wrote his phone number instead of his jersey number.

As Middle and Little participated in team sports, I watched thank-you gifts morph like team snack. Now, instead of a signed ball and a team photo, coaches were given gift cards loaded with $250. Toward the end of each sports season, I'd receive an email from the team parent, with "Shhh" in the subject line. The team parent was asking each family to donate $15 to $20, per coach, toward a gift card.

Days later, another email would arrive with "Shhh" in the subject line. *Had the team parent accidentally re-sent the email?* No. The coach was also requesting $15 to $20 toward a gift card for the team parent.

Michael and I had already spent $150 on registration, $60 on equipment, $100 on gas, $70 on snacks, $20 on a team photo, and $11 on a trophy. Thank-you gifts added another $45 to $60, and we'd spend at least $30 on pizza and drinks at the team party.

For years, we had at least two sons playing two sports, so I devised a simple multiplier to help with budgeting:

Registration Fee x 3.3

———

Does an out-of-town tournament count as a family vacation?

I live in San Diego with three million other people, but for reasons I don't understand, some of our youth sports teams are unable to find worthy opponents nearby. These teams travel far and wide to play other teams that are unable to find local opponents. Being on a travel team means a player's family has committed to spending an unknown number of weekends driving or flying to games and tournaments.

I once overheard a conversation between a dad, whose two daughters played on different travel teams, and another man, who sounded like he was a bachelor. The bachelor was trying to grasp the concept of a tourney trip.*

"So you and the family are goin' away this weekend?" the bachelor asked.

"Yeah, we have a soccer jamboree,*" said the dad.

"Are both girls playing?"

"Yeah. Samantha plays on Saturday morning, and Jessica plays on Sunday."

"So you leave Saturday morning?"

"No, we'll leave Friday afternoon. Samantha's game is at 7:30, but players have to check in by 6 a.m."

"And Jessica plays Sunday morning?"

---

tourney trip (*noun*): a brief getaway to attend a youth sports game or tournament.

soccer jamboree (*noun*): a poorly planned schedule of soccer games, which jams a family's weekend plans.

"No, afternoon—actually late afternoon. The game's at 4:00, but players have to be at the field by 2:30 for warm-ups."

"So after Saturday's game, what do you guys do 'til Sunday afternoon? Hang out by the pool?"

"Nah, the girls wanna shop. And go out to eat. Mostly shop."

"A whole weekend for two soccer games. What does that end up costing you, bro?"

"Uh, never really added it up. Let's see, two nights in a hotel, that's three hundred bucks. Self-parking, that's fifteen bucks a day. Eating out seven or eight times is like fifty bucks a meal—unless the girls bring teammates—then it's more. Game fees are thirty-five per player, so that's seventy for both girls. And maybe another seventy-five bucks in gas."

"You forgot shopping," said the bachelor.

"Okay, so another hundred bucks. What's that add up to?"

"About a grand. How often do you guys do this?"

"Not often, maybe six times a year."

"Bro, you spend six grand a year going to kids' soccer games?"

"Yeah I guess so. But all their friends are doing it. And it's time with the family."

"Dude, six grand."

Some families who have kids on travel teams are too busy (or broke) to take vacations, so they treat out-of-town games and tournaments as family fake-cations.* The key to enjoying some rest and relaxation, I've heard, is to avoid telling the kids they're on vacation. Wise parents wait until after the credit card statement arrives. With hard evidence in hand, it's easier to show kids how the family travel budget was blown on a weekend in Bakersfield.

———

fake-cation (*noun*): a non-leisure getaway that counts as a family vacation due to its cost, especially a college visit, a tourney trip, or an out-of-town graduation, wedding, or funeral.

How can I work out while my kids work out?

I've paid oodles in gym memberships to lift weights and walk on a treadmill. At the same time, I was paying oodles for my kids to play sports while I'd sit or stand for hours at practices and games. One day, I saw another mom walking laps on the track that surrounds the soccer field, so I joined her.

Now, while the kids practice or warm up for a game, I squeeze in some parkour: step-ups on the bleachers, push-ups against a picnic table, or bicep curls with a cooler. During a high school football game, I can cover five miles on the stadium's concourse.

 *WHAT THE AD SAYS:*

"A refreshing, year-round, heated clubhouse pool"

WHAT IT REALLY MEANS:

The clubhouse is heated. The pool is not.

After the season, do I throw away the team banner?

A team banner is the mascot, roster, and cheerleaders rolled into one work of art. By displaying a banner with bold colors and fancy graphics, a team is hoping to visually intimidate its opponents or at least divert their attention long enough to score.

I've been a banner manager, and it's an easy gig. Or rather, it was an easy gig. At the field, I'd hammer two Rebar spikes into the grass, set a frame of PVC pipes over the spikes, and attach the banner. Then artificial turf came along and complicated things. Spikes are prohibited on turf fields, so banner managers must now engineer and transport two types of displays.

After a banner has fulfilled its useful life of sixty days or so, it usually ends up in a local landfill where it takes who-knows-how-long to biodegrade. As new subdivisions are built atop old land-fills, it's possible that a resident with a pool-sized yard will dig deep enough during pool construction to hit a vein of team banners.

Were I still a banner manager, I'd treat the banner like a hand-me-down and pass it to next year's team. That team could quickly repurpose it by drafting players whose first names match the ones already on the banner and by using the same team name. Long live the Green Squirtles!

———

How do I deal with a pile of participation trophies?

Nothing reflects cookie-cutter culture like the gleam of a plastic participation trophy. Even if a team loses every game plus practice games, each player still receives a trophy. Yes, it's engraved like the Lombardi trophy. Yes, it's awarded at the team party. And yes, it's purchased by parents. From what I've seen, participation trophies come in three styles:

- The sports figurine atop a faux-marble platform
- The Olympic-inspired medal on a ribbon
- The understated commemorative pin

After years of having Big, Middle, and Little in youth sports, our collection of loving cups had runneth over. I'd known from the start that it was wrong to pay for a trophy and then award it to a kid as if he'd earned it, but the pressure to do so was strong.

Now, I found myself stashing commemorative pins and small medals to give out with our Halloween candy. Michael was making hat racks by unscrewing figurines and attaching them to a board, an idea I saw in *ReadyMade Magazine*. Had we not halted participation trophies, we might still be fashioning them into doorstops and garden statues.

I finally took a stand after Little's team ~~parent~~ manager had the players vote on which style of trophy they wanted to receive. Kids learn important values through team sports, but voting-to-receive sounded like vocational training for a career in politics. When the team manager emailed her standard request for trophy dough, I responded in a new way.

From: Marilyn (Danny's mom)
Subject: Award Party!!!!
Date: November 16
To: The Team

Hi All,

The boys voted to receive medals this year. We'll have the Award Party at Tony's Pizza after our game. I need to collect $11 from each of you for your son's medal.

Marilyn
Team Manager

From: Julie (Little's mom)
Subject: Re: Award Party!!!!
Date: November 16
To: Marilyn (Danny's mom)

Hi Marilyn,

No medal for Little, thank you. Sending regrets for the Award Party as well. We have the most fun at the games.

Thanks!
Julie

The next morning, on our drive to school, Middle and Little asked about trophies. I responded with a long-winded speech on trophies that are given and trophies that are earned. Middle, who was ten and had plenty of trophies, was fine with the new policy. Little, who was six and had zero trophies, fought back tears as he stepped out of the squirt hauler and headed to school.

At dinner, Michael and I reassured Little that he would some-day play in leagues that award real trophies. Suddenly, Middle left the table and darted upstairs. I could hear him fumbling around in his bedroom. Minutes later, he returned carrying four trophies that he was ready to give away. He asked Little which one he wanted. Little chose a trophy, and Michael made a label with Little's name and team name to fit over the existing plaque. Five minutes later, Little had lost interest in the trophy.

Would paying the eleven bucks have been easier? Maybe. But, subsidizing now could lead to higher costs later, such as paying a therapist to help our sons sort out why, as adults, they expect to be paid just for showing up at work rather than on how they perform. And what happens ~~if~~ when Big, Middle, and Little win major sports trophies? Will they ask how much I paid for them?

———

 WHAT THE AD SAYS:

"Brand new homes surrounded by highly rewarding surroundings"

WHAT IT REALLY MEANS:

Earn reward points at nearby supermarkets, gas stations, and retail stores.

7

Award-winning Schools

How can a brand new school have a full trophy case?

One reason we moved to a master-planned community was so Big, Middle, and Little could attend good schools. But the word *good* isn't good enough for subdivision builders, so they use terms like *acclaimed schools, premier schools, award-winning schools,* and *premier, award-winning schools.*

I assumed that all award-winning schools earned their awards after years of demonstrated excellence. Imagine my surprise when I walked into the lobby of a brand new school and found a nearly full trophy case. How was this possible?

I retraced the trophy trail, and it led back to the reward philosophy: reward participation, not performance. Like young athletes, award-winning schools also seem to receive awards for participating in the education process.

In my master-planned community, our K-6 elementary school was split into a K-4 elementary school and a 5-6 school school.* Slicing and dicing, I realized, creates more schools to garner more awards, a practice explained by the Three Core Values of cookie-cutter culture:

1. New

2. Convenient

3. Upgraded

Therefore, creating a **new** school is more **convenient** than **upgrading** an existing school.

---

school school (*noun*): an educational institution for fifth and sixth graders that is neither an elementary school nor a middle school.

Big, Middle, and Little each graduated from five schools: pre-school, elementary school, school school, middle school, and high school. Michael and I attended all fifteen graduation ceremonies.

―――

 *WHAT THE AD SAYS:*

"High-performing schools"

WHAT IT REALLY MEANS:

During standardized testing, parents are asked to pony up for catered lunches and shoulder massages, so students can perform at their best.

Is it healthier to drive or walk my kids to school?

The term *walking distance* connotes convenience, safety, and small-town charm. Michael and I chose our current subdivision partly because it was within walking distance of four schools.

I was thrilled to join a walking pool, where parents took turns escorting the peloton to and from the elementary school a mile away. I assumed that walking to school would let my sons take in some fresh air and exercise before they spent six hours inside a sealed building.

But the predominant odor on the way to school wasn't honeysuckle drifting on dewy morning air. It was a sickening mix of steamy car exhaust and scented dryer sheets. More fumes greeted my group when the sidewalk took us past the school valet lane.

Walking distance comes with a pollution paradox: kids who walk to school are probably exposed to more pollutants than kids who ride to school in gas-powered polluters.

———

WHAT THE AD SAYS:

"School-close living"

WHAT IT REALLY MEANS:

The subdivision is near a school (and a certain copywriter could use a refresher course on grammar).

Why do award-winning schools reward kids with candy?

Year after year, I'd sit in the dentist's waiting room and wonder why my kids were getting cavities, even though we limit sugar at home. The only evidence I had was the occasional Jolly Rancher candy wrapper that showed up in my washing machine. I assumed my kids were getting the candy from friends.

At the elementary school, one morning, I saw Little's Spanish teacher standing at the door to her classroom and holding open an old purse. Students were filing past her, mumbling "gracias," and then reaching into the purse to pull out a handful of candy. They devoured it within seconds. When I asked why she was handing out candy at 8 a.m., she said, "Students are supposed to save it for later." Clearly, something had been lost in translation.

When I showed the Jolly Rancher wrappers to Middle, he told me that Ms. Peterson (a parent who supervises the school playground) hands out Jolly Ranchers to kids who help put away the equipment after recess. I was tempted to send Ms. Peterson my dentist bills. When had candy replaced foil stars as a reward?

I was in the dentist's waiting room again when I overheard a dental assistant use the word *caries* instead of *cavities*. Suddenly, everything clicked! *Caries* must be a secret acronym for Candy As a Reward in Educational Settings. Eureka!

I started to recognize the CARIES Method everywhere. Not only were teachers using it but so was the school guidance counselor. When I asked why he was handing out candy after weekly meetings with the "strong-willed" kids, as he called them, he said,

"Even kids with temporary self-control issues need to be rewarded in a positive way."

Middle's piano teacher used the CARIES Method, too. After Middle had mastered a piece of music, his teacher opened the door to her coat closet and revealed a hanging shoe organizer filled with candy bars for students.

Banks, hair salons, and jewelry stores all used variations of the CARIES Method. So ubiquitous was this method that Michael and I established a Health Savings Account, so we could use pre-tax dollars to pay for any CARIES Method fallout, so to speak.

———

 WHAT THE AD SAYS:

"Acclaimed school district"

WHAT IT REALLY MEANS:

In terms of award-winning school districts, this is the runner-up.

Is there a specialty math class for subdivision kids?

I wonder why award-winning schools don't offer a specialty math class for subdivision kids. Such a class could teach kids to become more cautious consumers than their parents, who tend to charge everything to a credit card and pay it off with a home equity loan. Call it Sub Division 101, and teach real-life calculations like these:

- Security and pet deposits
- Square footages
- Good faith money
- Total housing cost (PITI* + HOA dues + Mello-Roos)

Where traditional math uses story problems, Sub Division 101 would use store problems since subdivision kids are more familiar with stores than stories.

Store Problem #1

Sherry's car needs 17 gallons of gas. The gas station offers three grades: regular ($4.19 per gallon), mid-grade ($4.29 per gallon), and premium ($4.39 per gallon). Sherry is paying by credit card, which adds a surcharge of 8 cents per gallon, and she wants to apply her grocery store reward points for a discount of 10 cents per gallon. She also wants to buy a $10 car wash. The clerk inside the gas station mini-mart needs to charge Sherry's credit card in advance of her purchase.

For each grade of gas, calculate the amount charged to Sherry's credit card.

---

* Principal, interest, property tax, insurance

Store Problem #2

Deena has a hair appointment at 3:30 p.m. Her three children, ages 7, 5, and 1, have a babysitter who earns $12.50 per hour. Deena needs to pick up the sitter at 2:20 and put the baby down for a nap by 2:45, so she can arrive with plenty of time to park her oversized SUV in the salon's tiny parking lot. The hairstylist charges $85, and Deena wants to include a 17% tip.

If Deena's hair appointment takes one hour and the baby sleeps for two hours, what time will Deena drive the sitter home?

How much will Deena pay the sitter?

How much will Deena pay the hairstylist?

📋 *WHAT THE AD SAYS:*

"Tech center"

✍ *WHAT IT REALLY MEANS:*

A space that's too small to be a bedroom but too big to be a closet—more like a fort with an electrical outlet, where kids can recharge.

Does my community have a school store?

Long before Apple and Google built corporate campuses, some large employers would operate a company store on their premises. A company store enabled employees to handle routine errands, like banking or dry cleaning, without leaving the workplace.

I'm hoping a tract home builder, or a stay-at-home parent who wants a side hustle, will soon see the benefits of opening a school store in my community. At the start of each school year, I'd visit the store's website and buy supplies for Big, Middle, and Little as pre-packaged bundles by grade level.

Kindergarten

- Napping mat
- Easy-to-open containers for snacks
- Valentine's Day cards that are free of commercial characters and weapons (including Cupid's arrow)

1st Grade

- Lightweight backpack
- Locking pencil box to reduce marker thefts
- Halloween costume that doesn't depict anything immoral, violent, or demeaning

2nd Grade

- Costume for Pioneer Days performance
- Fundraising catalog
- School-approved instrument for music class

3rd *Grade*

- School spirit T-shirt
- Bike lock to encourage biking to school
- Social Studies project materials and instructions to build a California mission or a Native American sweat lodge

4th *Grade*

- Costume for American History performance
- Pre-approved books for monthly book reports
- Room Parent's Venmo address and suggested donation to cover class parties, teacher's birthday gift, and year-end thank-you gift

5th *Grade*

- Pre-cut bedsheet and video instructions for making a toga
- Refrigerator magnet printed with computer passwords to access online textbooks
- One item from teacher's wish list (e.g., facial tissue, sticky notes, or printer paper)

6th *Grade*

- Packing list for 6th grade camp
- Calendar of Parent's Night Out activities for camp week
- Wardrobe guidelines for graduation ceremony

7th *Grade*

- P.E. uniform
- Trendy backpack
- Four pre-written notes to excuse student for orthodontist appointments
- Sturdy backpack for when trendy backpack fails in October

8th Grade

- Three P.E. uniforms in sequentially larger sizes to accommodate growth spurts
- Permission slip for year-end class trip
- List of local counselors specializing in adolescent behavior

9th Grade

- PSAT workbook and test dates
- Assignment organizer
- Reusable bag from high-priced boutique or hip restaurant to camouflage lunches from home

10th Grade

- Driver's permit requirements
- SAT workbook and test dates
- Pre-paid packages for winter and spring formals that include tickets, tux rental or spray tan, flowers, photos, dinner, and transportation

11th Grade

- Information on college scholarships
- Hotel discount codes for college visits
- Two-year prom package set up as monthly auto-withdrawal from checking account

12th Grade

- Order form for senior photos
- Grad Night ticket
- Yearbook
- Cap and gown
- Tickets to graduation ceremony

A school store would combine the convenience of a corner market, the discount prices of a big-box store, and the buy-back feature of a college bookstore, allowing costumes and graduation gowns to be reused.

———

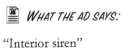 *WHAT THE AD SAYS:*

"Interior siren"

WHAT IT REALLY MEANS:

A whole-house alarm clock, so no one is late for work or school.

How will kids raised with automation learn to fix a toilet?

Lights come on when I enter a room. Car doors close at the push of a button. Toilets flush automatically. Sure, automation is nice, but what happens when kids raised with automation become renters or homeowners? Will they wonder why the shower stall is dirty, when the whole point of a shower is to get clean?

In my opinion, middle schools and high schools are uniquely positioned to prepare kids for a do-it-yourself future while also reducing the cost of campus maintenance. A course like Campus Care could bring in local, licensed experts to instruct students on basic plumbing, minor electrical tasks, and landscape maintenance. Graduating seniors would step into the real world with not only a diploma but also a list of trusted local contractors to call for help with painting, appliance repair, and mold remediation.

Campus Care doesn't strain school budgets. It stretches them. Schools could reduce costly service contracts by tapping the talent and energy of their student populations. Campus Care students would see the results of their efforts, take pride in their campus, and enjoy the self-confidence that comes from keeping one's surroundings clean, neat, and nice.

Does *foreign exchange* have to mean far away?

Foreign exchange programs offer students an exciting way to learn about history and culture. But for many families, including mine, the cost is out of reach. I wondered whether *foreign exchange* had to mean far away.

How about a floor-plan exchange program? I could send Big, Middle, or Little to live with a family in a different floor plan, subdivision, or master-planned community. They'd learn about local history and cookie-cutter culture through adventures like these:

- Sampling foreign fare at fast-food franchises that haven't expanded into our area.

- Encountering disruptive design elements, such as the morphing of wet bars into wine grottos.

- Enjoying exotic Common Area amenities, like streams and equestrian trails.

Like a foreign exchange, a floor-plan exchange would offer subdivision kids a chance to travel, meet new friends, and attend other award-winning schools.

———

📑 *WHAT THE AD SAYS:*

"Luggage shelves in garage"

✍ *WHAT IT REALLY MEANS:*

After you buy this home, you won't be doing much traveling.

8

Social Events

📝 1

Why do party hosts prefer paperless invitations?

In my master-planned community, paperless invitations appeal to all kinds of hosts, from those with eco egos* to Last-Minute Lucy, who plans her child's birthday party twenty-four hours in advance but schedules manicures in six-month blocks.

I assumed party hosts preferred paperless invitations for fast delivery and less waste. So why were hosts still loading up at the party store? They'd dig a carbon footprint the size of Sasquatch by buying cups, plates, napkins, utensils, tablecloths, balloons, loot bags, signs, streamers, centerpieces, confetti, candles, and piñatas.

I was chatting with the host of an upcoming party, when she mentioned that one guest had sent regrets. "That's okay," she said. "I can just email the invite to the next person on my list," almost as if she'd ranked her guests. Paperless invitations, I realized, provide hosts with social flexibility since paperless invitations don't require a rigid guest list, like paper invitations do. Paper invitations must be mailed all at once, so guests receive them at about the same time. A flexible guest list enables a host to divide guests into tiers of joy.* If a tier 1 guest sends regrets, a host can quickly backfill that hole in their guest list by emailing a tier 2 guest, without the fear of tier transparency.*

––––––

eco ego (*noun*): that part of the human psyche which is fed by saving the planet.

tiers of joy (*plural noun*): a rating that represents how happy one is in the presence of various people.

tier transparency (*noun*): a measure of openness about one's closeness with certain friends.

Is that a cell phone or a New Year's Eavesdropper?

On my street, neighbors party it up on New Year's Eve and party down* on New Year's Day. Walking to a New Year's Eve party is so much simpler than driving downtown. But when the kids were young, it was impossible to find a babysitter for the busiest night of the year. Michael and I would usually send one parent to the party while the other stayed home with the kids. Then we'd switch.

At one party, I noticed a younger couple who'd replaced their babysitter with technology. They had configured their phones as a New Year's Eavesdropper.* Here's how they did it:

Step 1: Set up a landline or a cell phone in baby's bedroom.

Step 2: From phone in baby's bedroom, call parent's phone.

Step 3: Answer parent's phone, and keep in ANSWER mode.

Step 4: Put baby to bed.

Step 5: Once baby is asleep, walk with phone, still in ANSWER mode, to New Year's Eve party.

I was talking with the younger mom about her sitter-less setup, when she abruptly put down her drink and dashed out of the party. Was the baby awake or had the call signal been dropped? I didn't know, but sooner than I expected, she was back.

---

party down (*verb*): to return to the home of last night's festivities in order to eat the leftovers and polish off the remaining booze.

New Year's Eavesdropper (*noun*): two phones that are connected and used to supervise a sleeping child on the one night a year when it's impossible to find a babysitter. (*Included for humor only. Do not attempt.*)

I wondered if the *sans*-a-yard* layout of our subdivision makes running from one house to another about the same distance as running from one end of a large custom house to the other end.

———

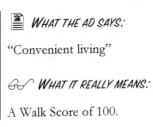 *WHAT THE AD SAYS:*

"Convenient living"

WHAT IT REALLY MEANS:

A Walk Score of 100.

---

sans-a-yard (*adjective*): without a yard.

Why does Presidents' Day last a week?

When Big was in elementary school, the district gave students one Monday off for President's Day, to honor the birthdays of two presidents who weren't born on the same day. In his English class, Big was learning that a plural possessive has an apostrophe after the "s."

When Middle was in elementary school, the district must have realized its error because it moved the apostrophe. Then it tacked on a Friday and dubbed the break "Presidents' Weekend." While Middle would've loved a three-day school week, the school calendar clearly showed that a weekend was two days long, not four.

By the time Little was in elementary school, the district had combined Presidents' Weekend, Valentine's Day, and three pupil-free days to create a nine-day break called Ski Week.

📄 *WHAT THE AD SAYS:*

"Inglenook"

✍️ *WHAT IT REALLY MEANS:*

The builder wants you to think you need one, even though you don't know what it is.

Can we afford a family vacation for Spring Break?

Spring Break is an ideal time for a family trip, but we're also on the hook for income taxes, property tax, and retirement contributions. Covering these *and* a family trip in the same month is a challenge, so I sometimes use hedge-fun investing.*

Around October, I book a family getaway for Spring Break by making airline and hotel reservations. To hedge my investment, I ensure that all reservations are fully refundable.

In March, I do a quick review of our finances to determine if we'll be taking a vacation or liquidating our leisure portfolio to pay bills. Depending on our destination, the cost of five round-trip tickets, lodging, and car rental can cover tax prep, tax payments, HSA contributions, prom expenses, summer camp deposits, and registration fees for fall sports.

———

WHAT THE AD SAYS:

"A home that reminds you of that vacation in Tuscany"

WHAT IT REALLY MEANS:

Each model has been staged with two wine glasses and a bottle of Chianti.

---

hedge-fun investing (*noun*): the practice of holding savings or emergency funds in refundable forms of leisure, especially airline tickets, which can be easily liquidated to pay bills.

Your friend got *what* in his Easter basket?

On Easter Sunday, it's common for the peloton to meet on the street and compare their baskets. One year, ten-year-old Middle dashed out the door with his basket but returned minutes later, looking glum. "Grant got a new baseball mitt," Middle said. The next year, Grant got a cell phone.

Easter's three-octave gift scale can create jealousy and confusion in the melting pot of sprawl-town kids. Added to the stew is the variety of holiday venues. While Jewish and Christian kids attend religious services and feast on traditional fare, other friends are inhaling fast food at the mall and shopping Spring Fling sales.

 *WHAT THE AD SAYS:*

"A euphoric home life"

WHAT IT REALLY MEANS:

A tangible home with intangible features

Why do strangers wish me a happy Mother's Day?

I was mulling over how to explain to Middle why Grant got a cell phone, when Mother's Day skidded in, and I caught myself comparing what I'd received to what other moms had received.

In cookie-cutter culture, Mother's Day kicks off a trinity of Hallmark holidays, when giving is more about obligation than inspiration. The Hallmark holidays seem to occur in descending order of commercialization with Mother's Day in May, Father's Day in June, and Grandparent's Day in September.

I'm always surprised when more than three people wish me a happy Mother's Day. I've received wishes from neighbors, baristas, grocery baggers, restaurant servers, and retail clerks. A real estate agent once mailed me Mother's Day wishes in a promotional piece.

Every so often, I'll hear of a spouse or a spousal equivalent who has upstaged a child's handmade card or craft for Mom with an OOPs gift.* It might be expensive jewelry, a major appliance, or a trip. Sometimes, an OOPs gift will mark a current holiday or special occasion *and* make up for a prior one that was overlooked or under-celebrated,* such as Valentine's Day, an anniversary, or a birthday.

———

OOPs gift (*acronym*): out-of-proportion gift; something given that is excessive in relation to the event it acknowledges, such as a major appliance for Mother's Day.

under-celebrate (*verb*): to acknowledge a holiday or a special occasion with a subpar level of pomp and celebration.

Why is Dad at the hardware store on Father's Day?

If Michael heads to the hardware store on Father's Day it's to finish the project he said would be done by Mother's Day.

———

 *WHAT THE AD SAYS:*

"Marvels of superb construction"

WHAT IT REALLY MEANS:

Even the builder is astonished at how these tract homes turned out.

On July 4th why do canopy owners ask non-relatives for help?

The July 4th block party in my subdivision celebrates freedom. At noon, when the barricades go up, kids are free to play in the street. They show up on bikes, trikes, roller skates, scooters, and skateboards. They ride with no hands and holding hands. They jump curbs and challenge each other to skid-mark contests.

Parents are freed from shouting, "Car!" Well, except for that one time when Mr. and Mrs. Meanie drove their luxury liner around the barricades. After neighbors stopped the car on the sidewalk, the Meanies whined that nobody had told them *when* the July 4th block party was.

Once the party perimeter is established, the infrastructure goes in: lawn chairs, ping-pong tables, a bounce house for the little kids, and rows of lightweight, folding banquet tables. To shade the potluck of Costco cuisine* that will grace these tables, neighbors haul out their pop-up shade canopies.

Seasoned canopy owners, I've noticed, recruit non-relatives for help with setup. This spreads the risk and cost of pinched fingers across several families. Plus, owners are more patient with a helpful neighbor who rips the canopy than they are with a family member who does the same.

With the party in full swing, neighbors, friends, co-workers, and relatives play games, eat, or linger at the Turf Club, a no-host bar fashioned from a potting bench and a piece of Astroturf.

Costco cuisine (*proper noun*): pre-packaged food from Costco that is passed off as homemade.

At dusk, after the barricades come down, we join people from the surrounding subdivisions for a mass pilgrimage up the hill to the view homes. There's a vacant lot at the end of a cul-de-sac where we can see five sets of fireworks.

The next morning, I join other early risers to sweep the street of Silly String, balloon pieces, and crushed Cheetos. Sometimes, I score a partying gift.*

———

 *WHAT THE AD SAYS:*

"Epicurean island-centerpiece kitchen"

WHAT IT REALLY MEANS:

The kitchen has an island.

---

partying gift (*noun*): something of value, such as clothing, a food storage container, or a serving piece, that is left behind after a social event and later claimed by a member of the cleanup crew.

Why do some kids skip recess before Grandparent's Day?

September brings a much-needed break from retail routines. I'm done with back-to-school shopping, and the winter holidays are months away. In keeping with this slower pace comes the last and least commercial Hallmark holiday: Grandparent's Day.

Although it's the newest holiday, it pays homage to the oldest relatives. Grandparent's Day was established with a proclamation by then-President Jimmy Carter in 1979, the same year the divorce rate peaked.

There is a connection. A high divorce rate leads to second and third marriages, which doubles and triples the number of grandparents a kid has. The week before Grandparent's Day, kids from blended families sometimes skip recess to finish cards and crafts for their fourteen grandparents.

———

🖼 *WHAT THE AD SAYS:*

"Enjoy 55+ adult living at The Falls"

👓 *WHAT IT REALLY MEANS:*

Every home comes with non-slip flooring.

Wait, the school wellness policy *doesn't* apply on Halloween?

Utter relief is what I felt one September when the school district introduced a wellness policy. Finally, administrators had taken a firm stance against the CARIES Method. Two months later, on Halloween, the school pushed aside the policy, so room parents could spread out an array of cookies, cupcakes, donuts, and fruit punch. "Change is slow," the principal told me.

The only benefit I see from this school-sponsored sugar fest is that it primes the (insulin) pump and readies kids for some after-school candy mapping. Candy mapping starts before dusk, when small groups of trick-or-treaters meet to map a route that maximizes their candy haul. In candy-mapping sessions, kids weigh the trade-offs between full-sized homes, snack-sized homes, and bite-sized homes. They consider physical obstacles, wardrobe malfunctions, and various modes of transportation.

Physical obstacles might be gate codes, courtyards, dim porch lighting, high vacancy rates, large dogs, and stairs. Wardrobe issues involve hats, wigs, shoes, swords, wings, wands, and props. Their transportation options are walking, running, biking, roller-skating, skateboarding, riding scooters, or having a parent drive. Candy mappers then crunch their data by asking questions:

- Will they net more candy by running to bite-sized homes or visiting fewer full-sized homes using rented golf carts?

- Can all witches cram their hats into their bike helmets?

- Where will they dump the first load of candy when their bags get too heavy?

Of course, there are black-swan events that the kids can't plan for, like when the Meanies handed out full-sized candy bars from their snack-sized home.

"Please take one."

Our circular subdivision is an ideal shape for trick-or-treating, so kids come from near and far on Halloween. When one neighbor ran out of candy, she used this simple trick to stay on good terms with trick-or-treaters: She closed her curtains and placed a chair under her porch light. She taped a sign above the chair that read, "Please take one." Then she set an empty bowl on the chair.

———

📄 *WHAT THE AD SAYS:*

"Meandering neighborhood pedestrian and bike pathways"

✍ *WHAT IT REALLY MEANS:*

The subdivision has sidewalks.

Did they pose for a holiday photo with another family's stuff?

One Thanksgiving, my family and I were at my sister's full-sized tract house when I found myself admiring her beautiful backyard: the sparkling pool, the leafy landscaping, and the mature trees. My backyard had none of this. I rounded up Michael and the boys, positioned us in front of some bougainvillea, and asked my dad to snap a few photos for our holiday card.

I've since learned that posing for a family photo with another family's stuff is fairly common in cookie-cutter culture. Whenever Big, Middle, and Little would attend a high school formal, they'd gather with friends beforehand, at a coveted residence, to await their limousine or party bus. Parents were also invited to this pre-party, mostly as paparazzi for teens dressed like celebrities.

I watched with curiosity as some party guests would wander off and pose for family photos next to high-end features in the host's home, such as a marble-like fireplace mantel or a stylish, painted wood stair system. During warm weather, families would pose next to the host's pool, pond, or fountain.

Family portraits taken by a professional can cost hundreds of dollars. These resourceful parents had eliminated that cost by squeezing more value from their semi-annual dance spend. I'd done the same by fitting in a family photo session at Thanksgiving. Since our holiday card goes only to out-of-town family members and friends, recipients don't know if what's in the background belongs to us or not.

———

Who stole my holiday decorations?

Every so often, someone on my street kicks off the holiday season with a game of Robbin' the 'Hood. To start, Neighbor #1 secretly swipes a holiday decoration from the front yard of Neighbor #2 and places it in the front yard of Neighbor #3. When the theft is discovered, a series of who-done-it emails or texts circulates until the identity of Neighbor #1 is revealed.

Although it's a seasonal game on my street, Robbin' the 'Hood can be played year-round with any exterior feature that isn't bolted down. Potted plants, patio furniture, flags, and trash cans all have potential as game pieces.

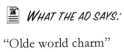

WHAT THE AD SAYS:

"Olde world charm"

WHAT IT REALLY MEANS:

The tract home's dirt yard and stark interior will whisk you back to life in the Middle Age.

Why are holiday letters so long?

The simple message behind every holiday letter is this:

Greetings! We're alive and well and living in _____.

But simplicity isn't a core value in cookie-cutter culture, which is why some letters are so long. From reading dozens of letters, I've spotted two best practices.

- BEST PRACTICE #1 -
Merge your circles.

A Venn diagram, for deciding who gets a holiday letter, looks like a solar eclipse. Writers merge their social circles by sending the same letter to everyone. The family dentist finds out what the family dog has been up to, and old friends are forced to read about how much fun the new friends are.

- BEST PRACTICE #2 -
Touch on every topic.

No topic is off limits. I've read about illness, aging relatives, trips, foreign languages spoken by kids under four, test scores, sports stats, diplomas, areas of study or promise for kids over eighteen, college degrees, promotions, hobbies, charitable projects, weight loss, concerts, plays, spiritual growth, and books. (Be sure to mention this one!)

The Four Components

A holiday letter has four components:

1. The greeting
2. The first sentence
3. The news
4. The closing

1. The Greeting

Some letters open with a line of poetry, a seasonal song lyric, or a favorite quote. Others use a broad, all-skate salutation like one of these:

Hi Everybody!

Dear Family and Good Friends,

Warm holiday wishes from _____!
(Writers who want to imply that they're on vacation will fill in the name of a resort destination.)

It's been awhile since we last sent greetings. We apologize.
('Tis the season for caring and sharing, so sharp writers share the blame by using the pronoun *we*.)

2. The First Sentence

The first sentence tells me what I'm about to dive into, whether it's good news, bad news, or no news.

We wish you and your family the best this holiday season!
(No news)

It's been a wonderful year, and we hope the same for you.
(Good news)

If the past year has taught us anything, it's that …
(Good news followed by bad news)

It's been a busy year.
(Good or bad news followed by better or worse news)

3. The News

Most writers allocate one paragraph per family member. This paragraph's first sentence sets the tone and reassures me that all is well with this family member, except when it's not.

Believe it or not, X is a really GOOD kid.
(She's fine.)

Y seems happily settled into dorm life.
(He's fine.)

We're savoring this year with X because we know it's the calm before the storm.
(She's living at home but has one foot out the door.)

We do our best to keep pace with Y and all of his activities.
(He's not around much, so we're plagiarizing this from his Facebook page and Twitter feed.)

X has built a solid foundation for herself.
(She's *still* living at home, so either she moves out or we do.)

Y continues to impress us with his …
(This kid is a damn handful, but we try to focus on the positives.)

The second sentence offers supporting details. Skillful writers hide any pride or disappointment by sticking to facts and avoiding adjectives.

X graduated with honors and earned scholarships to …
(Isn't she amazing?)

Y went to nationals this past year.
(You might have seen him on TV.)

X made the JV team.
(All that time and money we've spent is finally paying off.)

Y has grown six inches!
(According to the police lineup.)

From here, a family member's paragraph can take off in any direction. Below are some common words and phrases:

The highlight of ... family vacation ... soccer ... gymnastics ... piano lessons ... softball ... baseball ... school performance ... lacrosse ... basketball ... outstanding player ... all-star team ... competed in ... broke an arm ... speedy recovery ... good student ... has a part-time job ... college ... B.A. ... B.S. ... hit 40! ... The Big Trip ... high school reunion ... lost 23 pounds ... fabulous ... terrific ... the economy ... laid off ... back to school ... M.A. ... M.S. ... M.B.A. ... M.F.A. ... M.F.C.C. ... R.D. ... J.D. ... C.P.A. ... C.F.P. ... said goodbye to ... the cat ... our dog ... adorable kitten ... new puppy ... N.D. ... D.C. ... D.D.S. ... M.D. ... Ph.D. ... 50th birthday ... sold the house ... moved ... The Big Remodel ... college reunion ... lost 13 pounds ... 60th birthday ... surprise party ... diagnosed with ... continues to ... thankfully ... simple pleasures ... celebrated ... The Big Event ... so fortunate ... cruise ... skied ... the lake ... wine tasting ... grandchildren ... The Big 7-0 ... retired ... fishing ... volunteering ... wedding anniversary ... grown spiritually ... family reunion ... 80th birthday ... cancer ... our thoughts ... doing well at 95 ... many blessings.

4. The Closing

I've seen closings that are clever, religious, and holiday-themed. Some borrow from business correspondence, like *warmest regards*. Here are the most common closings I've seen:

Cheers!

Fondly,

Sincerely,

Best wishes,

Yours truly,

Have a blessed/warm/happy/safe holiday.

Blunders

Holiday letters are not without their blunders, especially if writers mention a social event that didn't include all readers. This is the downside of sending the same letter to everybody. One writer shared a big event and immediately pinned the responsibility on an unnamed party:

A handful of friends surprised Evelyn with a BIG birthday bash this past July.

A double-edged sentence like this leaves me conflicted. I feel left out but also guilty for not hosting my own bash for Evelyn. A different writer spun a big event as an impulsive, passionate act for which no one could be held accountable:

On our trip to Anguilla this year, Stan and I decided rather spontaneously to get married.

A phrase like *rather spontaneously* says, "Hope it's okay that we didn't invite you." Careful wording is also used to trot out one's success—be it financial, professional, or academic—in a year that devastated other readers. One tactful writer shared his success only after wishing readers similar success:

> Well, 2008 was a good year for me, and I hope 2009 will be a prosperous year for all of us.

The underlying message is, "I got mine, and I'm crossing my fingers that you'll get yours, too." Another writer acknowledged the prevailing economic conditions, but instead of mentioning his success outright, he mentioned only the trappings of it:

> Despite our nation's new fiscal policies, we're thankful for our many blessings, like our recent trip to see the Seven Wonders of the Ancient World.

To balance out bragging, some writers used bucket-list buffers to remind readers that the boasted-about achievement has been on the writer's bucket list for years. The implied message is, "It's not like I won the lottery. I've been planning this for a long time." Here are three popular bucket-list buffers:

> For as long as I can remember, I've always wanted to _____.

> Those closest to me know it's been a dream of mine to _____.

> As many of you know, I've always been passionate about _____, so I finally _____.

Postponements

A writer who postpones a holiday letter because the past year has been bad, busy, or boring can leave family members and friends in the lurch, wondering if they've been forgotten or even unfriended. I've seen two writers pull off postponements in a way that likely kept those relationships intact.

Both writers took a year off from writing a holiday letter, but they did send envelopes. In their letters the following year, both writers opened with an apology (or maybe a lie-pology), and they used the pronoun *we* to share the blame.

> *Writer 1*: To those of you who received an empty envelope last year, we apologize. We don't know how this happened.

> *Writer 2*: We were so busy last year that we finally hired an assistant. We've since learned that a few of you received empty envelopes. We're very sorry, and obviously, we're looking for a new assistant.

To lend credibility to their oversight, both writers shared two years' worth of news in their letters.

———

- CONCLUSION -

A Dream House

For too long, I entertained myself with the notion that living in a tract house was temporary, that these subdivisions were merely stops on my trajectory toward a dream house. Like my parents had done, Michael and I would eventually raise our kids in a custom house on a large lot. My dream house would have four bedrooms, a three-car garage, two home offices, a pool, a hot tub, fruit trees, a vegetable garden, a play structure, and dogs.

Yet here I was, decades later, still living in a tract house. Destiny had clearly disagreed with my master plan. I imagined what Destiny might have said, had She sat me down years ago for a frank talk about this whole dream-house thing.

"I found you a house," She would say, Her voice higher on the last word. "It's not a custom house, and it's not on a large lot, but it does have the four bedrooms you wanted. It's a 1986 Tudor-inspired tract house on almost one-eighth of an acre. The walls and ceiling are covered in orange-peel texture, there's white carpet everywhere except in the wet bar, and the master bedroom has pink-striped wallpaper straight out of an ice cream shop.

"But," Destiny would hold up an index finger to signal good news. "The floor plan has an invisible loop that passes through the kitchen, the living room, and the family room. Big, Middle, and Little will chase each other endlessly around that loop and shriek with laughter. Sometimes Nerf guns will be involved. Sometimes you'll be involved. Your house will be filled with laughter and running, even though these weren't on your wish list.

"The house doesn't have a three-car garage," Destiny would say. "It has a two-car garage that will barely fit a bicycle after your stuff is moved in. Even when the boys start driving and you have three cars, you will still have a two-car garage with no cars in it.

"But, that garage will be a godsend. When Michael is laid off and starts a new business, the garage will be his warehouse. When Big, Middle, and Little want to hang out with friends, they'll hang out in the garage. In 2009, when the Great Recession closes your local gym with no warning, you, Michael, and Tony Horton will cobble together a garage gym. In 2020, when a pandemic closes every gym on the planet, you'll be so grateful for that garage gym.

"Now, about those home offices, yours will be a mobile office since you'll be moving it from a dining area to a bedroom to a walk-in closet to a backyard shed. You'll love the shed. Except on weekdays when gas-powered leaf blowers fill the air with exhaust from yards so far away you can't even see them. You did forget to put fresh air on your wish list, but luckily, I snagged you some. On Sunday mornings, when those gardeners are sleeping or at church, you'll have a few hours of fresh air. Take a long deep breath. Then hold it. For six days.

"Okay, so you also want a pool, a hot tub, fruit trees, a play structure, a vegetable garden, and dogs. Guess what? You can have it all!

"But you won't. You said it yourself: Dogs need space to run. So, no dogs for now. And honestly, a pool and a hot tub will take up your entire backyard. Do you want to commute by kayak to your office shed? Of course you don't. So, the backyard will host the play structure, and the front yard will host the fruit trees. Once the boys outgrow the play structure, you and Michael will rip out the lawn and replace it with a vegetable garden. You'll grow more food than you thought possible. And when you see how many vegetables the boys *don't* eat, you'll build a compost bin. That bin will divert one ton of vegetables away from the landfill."

Destiny would take a cleansing breath and then say, "Alright, that takes care of your list, but I have something to add: neighbors. The tract house I found for you is ten feet from the houses on either side. One of those will become a rental. Boy, will you meet all kinds of people when that home is a rental for fifteen years. Single people. Married people. Single people who act married. Married people who act single.

"The houses are packed so tightly that thirteen windows will have a view into your backyard. You'll have a view into neighbors' yards as well, which is good because the boys will launch a lot of stuff into those yards. One son will break a window, another will lose every single Stomp Rocket, and the third will crash his drone on a neighbor's roof.

"But," Destiny would pause for emphasis. "Who will help you repair your fence when the HOA won't? Who will carpool with you to school and sports? Who will welcome your kids into their homes and care for them like their own? Who will invite your family to play cards by candlelight during blackouts? Who will host Bunco, poker night, and happy hour? Who will throw block parties every July 4th and white-elephant gift parties every holiday season? Who will celebrate New Year's Eve at 9 p.m.? Who will post hundreds of photos of all the fun?" Destiny would wink, smile, and disappear. I'd always thought of a dream house as having everything. I never considered what it might be missing.

One day, like so many others, I'd had enough of subdivision living. Enough of leaf blowers, cramped yards, and air tinged with scented detergent and delivery-truck diesel. So I took a dream-house drive. Years had passed since my last one. In those wealthy neighborhoods, the homes were just as gorgeous and just as pricey as ever. Where Younger Me had swooned over a hoped-for future, Older Me was thinking more practically now. I thought about property taxes, utility bills, and giant mortgages. I imagined the hassle of having to drive everywhere—to playdates, to school, to sports, to the grocery store. How much time and money would Michael and I have spent to furnish, clean, repair, remodel, and insure such a stately house?

But look at those huge lots. No side yards. No solicitors. No HOA telling me what I can and can't do.

The sprawling lawns were green, tidy, and empty. Basketball hoops, trampolines, and tennis courts stood quiet. The occasional luxury car sped past, always too fast. In spite of San Diego's world-famous weather, the only people outside appeared to be gardeners.

My gaze settled on a modest mansion that fit my earlier wish list. The house held my attention for only a few seconds before I caught myself looking at the houses on either side and wondering, *Who would my neighbors be?*

I headed back toward my master-planned community with its coveted residences, pool-sized yards, award-winning schools, and convenient shopping. At my welcome wall, I turned right and saw kids riding bikes, parents pushing strollers, and neighbors walking dogs. We waved. As I rounded the corner, I saw a group of teenagers playing basketball on a freestanding hoop in the street, and I knew which house was mine.

———

GLOSSARY

A

advertised feature (*noun*): an element that receives top billing in marketing materials: *walking distance, close-knit community.*

airshot (*noun*): the distance over which an odor can be detected. *I can smell the nauseating scent of Wanda's dryer sheets because our homes are within airshot.* See ODOR ALIGNMENT.

all-skate (*adjective*): inclusive of everyone.

Amazon Prime parking (*proper noun*): a strategy by which the driver of an unmarked van can park almost anywhere by leaving an Amazon box on the dashboard and exiting the vehicle wearing a fluorescent orange vest.

B

backyard pool (*noun*): a water feature that engulfs the entire rear yard of a tract house. See POOL-SIZED YARD.

BFF (*abbreviation*): best floor-plan friend; an acquaintance who occupies the same bedroom in the same floor plan as you do. See FLOOR-PLAN FRIEND.

big-city bedroom (*noun*): in a tract home, a bedroom the size of a dinky, downtown apartment bedroom; often, a college-prep bedroom occupied by a college grad. See COLLEGE-PREP BEDROOM.

bite-sized home (*noun*): a condo or townhouse; named for the candy bar size that trick-or-treaters expect. See CANDY MAPPING, FULL-SIZED HOME, and SNACK-SIZED HOME.

bucket-list buffer (*noun*): a phrase used to balance out bragging, especially in a holiday letter: *a lifelong dream, a passion of mine.*

C

candy mapping (*verb*): the act of determining which trick-or-treat route will yield the biggest haul of candy. See BITE-SIZED HOME, FULL-SIZED HOME, and SNACK-SIZED HOME.

CARIES Method, the (*acronym*): candy as a reward in educational settings; a common motivational tool used by teachers, guidance counselors, coaches, playground supervisors, and others who work with children.

clothing cave (*noun*): a storage space advertised as a walk-in closet, which becomes cramped and dark after an actual wardrobe is moved in; may require minor spelunking to coordinate an outfit or find matching shoes.

college-prep bedroom (*noun*): in a tract home, a bedroom the size of a dorm room. See BIG-CITY BEDROOM.

compatible uses (*plural noun*): identical, similar, or harmonious functions in neighboring side yards: *compost heap | vegetable garden; chicken coop | fruit trees; barbecue | smoker.* See COMPROMISED USE, INCOMPATIBLE USES, and SIDE YARD.

compromised use (*noun*): receiving less than the full potential from one's side yard, due to a more offensive use occurring in the neighboring side yard. See COMPATIBLE USES, INCOMPATIBLE USES, and SIDE YARD.

convenience curb (*noun*): a red, yellow, blue, or green street curb used by drivers who believe they are too busy to park in a marked stall.

cookie-cutter (*adjective*): identical, as though pressed or cut from the same mold.

coping cost (*noun*): an expense related to the stress of living next to a construction site; usually incurred by buyers in the early phases of a subdivision as they await completion of the remaining phases.

Costco collectible (*proper noun*): an item once purchased at Costco but never available again.

Costco cuisine (*proper noun*): pre-packaged food from Costco that is passed off as homemade.

D

deckumentary (*noun*): a short film that documents the professional decorating process used to deck out model homes.

dining area (*noun*): a space for eating that is adjacent to, or within, another room having a non-dining function, such as a living room or a great room.

dining nook (*noun*): a space for eating that has just enough floor area to accommodate two folding chairs and a wall-mounted table.

dining room (*noun*): a space for eating that has three to four walls, a chandelier, and a window.

doo dodger (*noun*): one who avoids cleaning up after one's pet.

double cul-de-sac (*noun*): two adjacent dead ends, which form a street configuration resembling Mickey Mouse's ears; also, the most sought-after street configuration in a subdivision.

E

early-phase equity (*noun*): the value of ownership in a new tract home that can be attributed to price increases in subsequent phases of the subdivision.

eco ego (*noun*): that part of the human psyche which is fed by saving the planet: *Sending paperless invitations feeds my eco ego.*

estate-sized yard (*noun*): an invented amenity that describes an under-landscaped or unmaintained backyard used by the residents to store items that don't fit in the house. See FAMILY-SIZED YARD, INVENTED AMENITY, and POOL-SIZED YARD.

F

fake-cation (*noun*): a non-leisure getaway that counts as a family vacation due to its cost, especially a college visit, a tourney trip, or an out-of-town graduation, wedding, or funeral. See TOURNEY TRIP.

family-sized yard (*noun*): an invented amenity that describes an under-landscaped or unmaintained backyard having a flat, bare spot suitable for an accessory dwelling unit to house a relative. See

ESTATE-SIZED YARD, INVENTED AMENITY, and POOL-SIZED YARD.

feature finesse (*noun*): the ability to identify subtle differences between similar-sounding home elements. See DINING AREA, DINING NOOK, DINING ROOM, LAUNDRY AREA, LAUNDRY CENTER, LAUNDRY ROOM, and LAUNDRY STADIUM.

-flavored (*suffix*): a term combined with a color name to specify one's choice of sports drink: *Mom, can you get me red-flavored Gatorade at the snack bar?*

floorclosure (*noun*): being unable to pay the mortgage after overspending on upgrades; characterized by a house where everything has been upgraded except the floors.

floor-plan exchange program (*noun*): a foreign exchange program modified for students in subdivisions.

floor-plan friend (*noun*): an acquaintance who lives in the same floor plan as you do. See BFF.

full-sized home (*noun*): a large, detached tract house; named for the candy bar size that trick-or-treaters expect. See BITE-SIZED HOME, CANDY MAPPING, and SNACK-SIZED HOME.

funeral home (*noun*): the residence that one expects to live in until death.

G

Graduated Shopping Requirements (*proper noun*): a set of guidelines to safely emancipate teenage shoppers from the embarrassment of shopping with an adult.

guessed suite (*noun*): a guest bedroom and bathroom where a host has eliminated all guesswork as to how long a guest is welcome, usually by placing an obstacle to the guest's comfort, such as a cat litter box in the bathroom or too many mothballs in the closet.

H

hedge fund (*noun*): money earmarked for the purchase of fencing and/or plants, usually with the intent of increasing privacy.

hedge-fun investing (*noun*): the practice of holding savings or emergency funds in refundable forms of leisure, especially airline tickets, which can be easily liquidated to pay bills.

HELOC (*acronym*): home equity line of credit; a source of borrowed money used to pay for home improvements or lifestyle enhancements, such as a luxury car, fancy jewelry, or an elaborate trip.

houndary (*noun*): the boundary where dogs are welcome to pee, poop, play, and explore; typically includes the Common Area in a subdivision and excludes front yards.

houndsight (*noun*): a revised perception of the nature of a dog; usually marked by the discovery of an annoying habit.

house-trained (*adjective*): the ability to identify one's look-alike home without the aid of an electronic device, a photo, or a document.

I-J-K

incompatible uses (*plural noun*): inharmonious functions in neighboring side yards: *pool heater* | *meditation garden*; *pesticide* *storage | playhouse; beehive | tanning area.* See COMPATIBLE USES, COMPROMISED USE, and SIDE YARD.

-influenced/-inspired (*suffix*): identifies a faux feature: *The Bellevue floor plan has wood-inspired window frames.* See -LIKE, -STYLE, and STYLING.

invented amenity (*noun*): a basic feature that goes by an enticing name in advertising materials: *an estate-sized yard.* See ESTATE-SIZED YARD, FAMILY-SIZED YARD, and POOL-SIZED YARD.

L

laundry area (*noun*): a dedicated-but-doorless space for a side-by-side washer and dryer, which is adjacent to, or within, another space having a non-laundry function, such as a garage, a mudroom, or a kitchen.

laundry center (*noun*): a closet containing a stackable washer and dryer; usually found behind bifold doors in a hallway or kitchen.

laundry room (*noun*): a space having four walls and a door and which functions solely as a place for clothing care.

laundry stadium (*noun*): an oversized space having two sets of commercial-sized washers and dryers, a folding counter the length of a sports bar, a refrigerator, and a wide-screen TV.

lie-pology (*noun*): a fib combined with an apology.

-like (*suffix*): describes a wanna-be feature: *a country club-like setting.* See -INFLUENCED/-INSPIRED, -STYLE, and STYLING.

M

Mello-Roos (*proper noun*): a rather hefty tax typically attached to tract homes in special districts, for at least 20 years, to fund public improvements; a variation of *mellow ruse*, meaning to trick or deceive in a relaxed and pleasant way. See ROOS AND THE DUES, THE.

me-mergency (*noun*): a subjective measure of severity.

mid-makeover (*adjective*): the state of being in the middle of a home remodeling project: *Harriet's kitchen is mid-makeover.*

mow 'n blow (*noun*): a brief service call made by a team of gardeners to mow the lawn and blow the leaves. See TEN-MINUTE TORNADO.

my model (*noun*): a reference made by the buyer of a new tract home to the model home with the same floor plan: *The Windsor floor plan is my model.*

N

neighborhood neutrality (*noun*): the bland color palette of a typical subdivision, emanated by earth-toned houses, brown roofs, and beige walls.

New Year's Eavesdropper (*proper noun*): two phones that are connected and used to supervise a sleeping child on the one night a year when it's impossible to find a babysitter.

noise alignment (*noun*): the practice of generating noise when a neighbor within earshot is also generating noise. See ODOR ALIGNMENT.

noise credit (*noun*): an imaginary allotment of ruckus that neighbors within earshot agree to tolerate for a specific time period.

O

odor alignment (*noun*): the practice of generating an odor when a neighbor within airshot is also generating an odor. See AIRSHOT and NOISE ALIGNMENT.

OOPs gift (*acronym*): out-of-proportion gift; something given that is excessive in relation to the event it acknowledges, such as a major appliance for Mother's Day.

original owner (*noun*): a buyer who purchases a new tract home directly from the builder: *I wonder what the original owner paid for this house.*

ornamentally challenged (*adjective*): a seasonal decorative disorder marked by the inability to acceptably decorate the curbside exterior of one's home, especially during the winter holidays. See UNDER-DECORATE.

our owners (*plural noun*): a reference made by the present owners of a tract home to the home's previous owners: *We didn't install the granite countertops. Our owners did that.*

P-Q

paparazzi party (*noun*): a social gathering of high school students and their parents, for the dual purposes of awaiting a limousine and taking photos before a prom or other formal dance: *For this year's holiday card, we took our family photo at a paparazzi party.*

participation trophy (*noun*): a trinket given to every player on a team, regardless of the team's win-loss record.

party down (*verb*): to return to the home of last night's festivities in order to eat the leftovers and polish off the remaining booze.

partying gift (*noun*): something of value, such as clothing, a food storage container, or a serving piece, that is left behind after a social event and later claimed by a member of the cleanup crew.

Party Plan, the (*slang*): the largest floor plan in a subdivision. See PLAN 4.

pebble promo (*noun*): a plastic baggie containing a few small rocks and a business card or a flyer.

pee-requisites (*plural noun*): the elusive set of pre-conditions that dogs require before they'll tinkle on something: *I'm surprised that fake grass meets Fido's pee-requisites.*

petiquette (*noun*): short for *pet etiquette*; the socially acceptable behaviors and choices of pet owners.

Plan 4 (*slang*): the largest floor plan in a subdivision. See PARTY PLAN, THE.

pleasement (*noun*): in a sardine-packed subdivision, the unofficial right of non-owners to use vacant private property, such as a driveway or a front lawn, for their own enjoyment.

pocket park (*noun*): a small grassy area in a subdivision.

pool-sized yard (*noun*): an invented amenity that describes an under-landscaped or unmaintained backyard that supposedly holds vast potential. See BACKYARD POOL, ESTATE-SIZED YARD, FAMILY-SIZED YARD, and INVENTED AMENITY.

post-purchase discovery (*noun*): any aggravating design flaw that a buyer overlooked on the model tour and must now live with.

power trip (*noun*): a free or low-cost vacation alternative: *Madge couldn't afford a vacation, so she took a power trip by citing a neighbor for setting out his trash cans too early.*

preview party (*noun*): an informal social gathering, held as a progressive event the night before a neighborhood garage sale, where neighbors participate in the Stuff Sackrament. See STUFF SACKRAMENT.

privacy barrier (*noun*): a one-foot-tall panel of lattice or angled wood slats that extends the height of an existing, HOA-compliant fence and results in a see-through fence at eye level.

R

reach-in (*adjective*): often describes a walk-in closet or pantry that loses its walk-in rating after an average amount of clothing or food is moved into it. See SQUEEZE-IN.

rebeloquence (*noun*): the ability to persuasively express a counterpoint.

RELOC (*acronym*): rookie-roost equity line of credit; a source of borrowed money used to pay for improvements to a rookie roost or for lifestyle enhancements, such as trendy electronics, concert tickets, or expensive clothes. See HELOC and ROOKIE ROOST.

Robbin' the 'Hood (*proper noun*): a game in which one neighbor secretly swipes something from a second neighbor's front yard and places it in the front yard of a third neighbor.

rookie roost (*noun*): an accessory dwelling unit where a future homeowner can learn about basic repairs, routine maintenance, and regular payments. See RELOC.

roos and the dues, the (*slang*): Mello-Roos and HOA dues. See MELLO-ROOS.

Rule of Three, the (*proper noun*): a cookie-cutter corollary, which states, If one resident does it, two neighbors will also do it: *If one resident installs new windows, two neighbors will also install new windows.*

S

sans-a-yard (*adjective*): without a yard.

school school, a (*noun*): an educational institution for fifth and sixth graders that is neither an elementary school nor a middle school: *Cole attends River Ranch School School.*

side yard (*noun*): a strip of dirt in between tract houses, where the scaffolding once stood. See COMPATIBLE USES, COMPROMISED USE, and INCOMPATIBLE USES.

snack camp (*noun*): a picnic blanket, wagon, or collapsible table from which a snack family serves halftime and post-game snacks to participants at a youth sports game. See SNACK FAMILY.

snack family (*noun*): a team member's immediate relatives who are assigned to bring a smorgasbord of halftime and post-game goodies to a youth sports game. See SNACK CAMP.

snack-sized home (*noun*): a mid-sized, detached tract house; named for the candy bar size that trick-or-treaters expect. See BITE-SIZED HOME, CANDY MAPPING, and FULL-SIZED HOME.

soccer jamboree (*noun*): a poorly planned schedule of soccer games, which jams a family's weekend plans.

squeeze-in (*adjective*): describes a space, such as a guest bathroom, that requires a person to turn sideways to enter or use the space. See REACH-IN.

squirt hauler (*noun*): the family car.

Stuff Sackrament, the (*proper noun*): a cherished ritual held before a neighborhood garage sale, during which neighbors in different life stages buy and sell used goods, to ensure that the best stuff never leaves the neighborhood. See PREVIEW PARTY.

-style (*suffix*): describes an imposter feature; the hyphen (-) functions like a minus sign: *a resort-style pool* (a pool minus the resort). See -INFLUENCED/-INSPIRED, -LIKE, and STYLING.

styling (*noun*): an upgraded, stand-alone version of *-style*, meant to add richness and intrigue: *The kitchen boasts decorator touches of Tuscan styling.* See -INFLUENCED/-INSPIRED, -LIKE, and -STYLE.

supply sensor (*noun*): an internal alert that, when triggered, causes one to add an item to one's shopping list.

T

ten-minute tornado (*noun*): the rage-inducing noise and toxic air generated by a team of gardeners using gas-powered lawn mowers and leaf blowers. See MOW 'N BLOW.

Three Core Values, the (*proper noun*): the tenets most cherished in cookie-cutter culture: New, Convenient, and Upgraded.

tiers of joy (*plural noun*): a rating that represents how happy one is in the presence of various people.

tier transparency (*noun*): a measure of openness about one's closeness with certain friends.

tourney trip (*noun*): a brief getaway to attend a youth sports game or tournament. See FAKE-CATION.

tree-quivalent (*noun*): a tall, fabricated object that functions visually like a tree but requires little or no maintenance, such as a flagpole, a lamp post, an owl box, or a freestanding basketball hoop.

U

ulterior designer (*noun*): a subdivision resident who lies about or conceals the source of furniture, flooring, décor, and the like, with the hope of having a unique home.

under-celebrate (*verb*): to acknowledge a holiday or a special occasion with a subpar level of pomp and celebration.

under-decorate (*verb*): to display few, if any, holiday decorations on a home's curbside exterior. See ORNAMENTALLY CHALLENGED.

V

vet-together, a (*noun*): an informal social gathering held in a model home for the purpose of identifying deficiencies in the floor plan: *I hosted a vet-together in my model, and Hazel discovered that this floor plan has no water spigot on the patio.* See MY MODEL.

W-X-Y-Z

weekly walk-through (*noun*): a recurring visit to the same model home for the purposes of taking measurements, stealing decorating ideas, and locating defects; *conjugations*: bi-*weekly walk-through*, tri-*weekly walk-through*.

welcome wall (*noun*): a short, horizontal masonry structure at the entrance to a subdivision, which displays the subdivision's name.

wilderness premium (*noun*): a surcharge on the price of a new tract home, which supposedly reflects the home's prime location as having a view of nature.

window permit (*noun*): an official-sounding, but non-existent, building requirement; occasionally used on April Fool's Day or by people taking a power trip. See POWER TRIP.

ACKNOWLEDGMENTS

I'm grateful to the following people for their help in bringing this book to life and for bringing life to this book:

My neighbors—past and present—for their friendship, hospitality, and sense of humor.

Ashley, Bennett, Brian, Carsen, Erin, Jackson, Jake, Jan, Jim, Kim, Laura, Louisa, Pam, Wig, and Woods for their feedback.

Patrece, for her edits and a steady stream of encouragement.

Mom, for her love of houses and her eye for detail.

My sister, for her beautiful homes and yards.

My brother, for his rebeloquence.*

Big, Middle, and Little, for our many shared adventures.

Michael, for his love and support and for all those home-cooked dinners delivered to my office shed.

———

---

rebeloquence (*noun*): the ability to persuasively express a counterpoint.

A NOTE FROM JULIE

Thank you for reading, scrolling, or flipping through this book. If you enjoyed the book, consider leaving a review on Amazon, Goodreads, or wherever you like to post reviews.

To share this book with neighbors, floor-plan friends, or your real estate agent, consider sending the e-book edition by visiting your favorite e-book retailer.

Reach me at julie@juliewheaton.com.

CPSIA information can be obtained
at www.ICGtesting.com
Printed in the USA
FSHW021554220421
80628FS